ARE WE OLD YET?

A CASUAL CONVERSATION ABOUT AGING

GARRY COLE

Are We Old Yet?
A casual conversation about aging

ISBN: 979-8-9887304-0-8 (Paperback Edition)
ISBN: 979-8-9887304-1-5 (Ebook Edition)

For permission requests please email garry@garrycole.com
or visit www.garrycole.com.

Although this publication is designed to provide
accurate information in regard to the subject matter
covered, the publisher and the author assume no
responsibility for errors, inaccuracies, omissions, or any
other inconsistencies herein. This publication is meant
to be a source of valuable information for the reader,
however it is not meant as a replacement for direct expert
assistance. If such level of assistance is required, the
services of a competent professional should be sought.

To my family, whom I love:
May you be happy, healthy, and live a long life.

TABLE OF CONTENTS

IMPORTANT BACKSTORY

As I grow older, I love to reminisce. And why not? It's like reading a book with me as the main character, and I get to control the storyline and the ending. Some reminiscences are happy, and some, sadly, are not. Memories, like a good library, will grow over time and are one of the many things that change as we age. If you're like me, you enhance the good ones and forget the bad ones. I mean, we don't keep bad books, do we? I find myself going back to my favorites time and time again.

One of those favorites is Family Camp. For many years, my wife and I would pack up the kids to make the three-hour drive to Oscoda, Michigan. Family Camp was Labor Day weekend at the YMCA Camp and a fun way to end the summer—the closest my wife was ever going to get to actual camping. Here we had a cabin, planned activities, and meals provided—the only way to camp, she would say, and say often.

The first year we went, the kids were young but old enough to understand, remember, and enjoy the activities. It was the first real road trip for them. And the first time I heard the infamous words "Are we there yet?" The drive was uneventful, the best kind with two young ones in the back seat. Well, uneventful until we got into Oscoda . . . so close. My son started to complain of stomach pain and asked that we pull over. Not one to push my luck, I pulled over in the Burger King parking lot, not the best location as it would turn out. My son jumped out of the car and vomited like it was his first time drinking a pitcher of margaritas made with cheap tequila. It wasn't tequila, and he was six. Not knowing the cause of said stomach ailment, we journeyed on to camp, just a short five-minute drive down the road. Let me apologize to BK; we drove off without any effort to clean up, my bad. As you may have guessed, this is not a good part of the memory.

We arrived at camp with Parker looking a bit green around the gills. We didn't know if we would stay, given the recent incident at BK, but we needed a place for the night, so we checked in at camp.

Our cabin was a 10-minute walk from the car, so I hoisted Parker onto my shoulders for the trip. As we walked, you could see Parker's mood start to change. You could feel his excitement as he saw the lake, the woods, and all the other families kicking balls and playing ga-ga ball, a variation of dodgeball, which would become a favorite activity. And then, just before we arrived at our cabin, Parker shouted, "Today is the first best day ever."

* * *

First best day ever? He had just left the contents of his stomach in a parking lot 15 minutes earlier. How could this be a good day, let alone the best day ever?

2

It's those words of a six-year-old that have had a dramatic effect on how I approach aging. Please allow me to introduce myself. My name is Garry Cole. I'm not famous. I'm the father of two wonderful kids, now in college and medical school (when I wrote this), respectively, and husband of a loving wife who still has never camped in a tent in her life. I'm not a doctor, scientist, psychiatrist, nutritionist, or gerontologist. I'm a person who is on an aging journey, just like you.

My interest in the aging process was somewhat career-driven as I worked in the industry for a number of years. Let me give a shout-out to the Area Agency on Aging, my employer, and a wonderful resource for people who can use some help in finding solutions for the multiple challenges that may occur in the aging process.

My real passion, however, is driven by a personal story. Like many of you, I watched both of my parents age and eventually pass. Their journeys were different. They were dealt different hands, with unique opportunities and challenges. My role was different with each of them because of the circumstances. If given the chance, I would have been more involved with both of them. They were my parents, and my parents deserved more.

Now I find myself in uncharted territory as I enter a time in my life when so many things are changing, some good, some not so good. I thank God at the end of each day and pray that I will wake up for the next. And every day I'm reminded of the words of a six-year-old boy, "Today is the first best day ever."

That's why I wrote this book. I wanted to remember the past and, more important, prepare for the future. Would my journey end in a nursing home—as my mom's did for four years and my dad's for one—or do I have options? Can I influence this journey? Can I make it better? After all the research, the short answer is yes.

We each have a unique set of circumstances, but the daily choices we make in our lives can play a significant role regardless.

So, let's have a casual conversation about aging and find ways to make this "the first best day ever" or as close as it can be.

ABOUT THE BOOK

I wrote this book for myself but humbly would like to share it with you. As I got older, I wanted to know. I wanted to know everything about aging: what to expect, whether it's as bad as we are all led to believe, and if there is anything I can do about it. Is there a fountain of youth?

So I started my research, lots of research—hundreds of articles, books, podcasts, and documentaries about aging, every aspect of aging. What I learned was, yes, life is going to change. It can be bad, very bad. I originally considered naming my book *Getting Old Sucks*. However, I didn't think people would read a book with that name, and I didn't want to write that book.

I like to focus on the good we can find in life. There is much we can do to make this journey better and even good in many circumstances. Or, at the very least, good, relative to how bad we thought getting old was going to be.

The other thing I learned is there is no shortage of information. Much research has been done in the last 30 years about why and how we age. Although not all the science is perfectly aligned, we do know what causes aging and even ways to slow it down, deal with it, and make life better. That's what I wanted to know—how we can make the best of our time here on earth.

I wanted to share this information, my research from reading the work of others, and share some of my personal stories and thoughts in the hope that you may benefit and live your best life possible as well.

If there is so much written about aging, why do we need another book on the subject? Fair question. There are many books currently on the market, many great books, well written and informative. I would encourage you to read as many as you can. This book is different. It's a "casual conversation" with a mix of science, nostalgia, and personal stories. More of a light read with some attempts at humor just for fun.

I'm not looking to change the world or even your life. If I have an impact on your day, make you smile, think, or even learn something that may have a positive influence on your aging journey, that would be enough for me.

I will be jumping around a bit, covering many topics, from identity to happiness, with 35 separate conversations in total. I suspect you may like some more than others, but isn't that how conversations go? The one unifying factor is aging. Yes, a casual conversation about aging. So think of each conversation as coffee with friends. Conversations tend to wander. One minute you may be solving the world's problems, and the next, you may be asking yourself, Am I old yet? There may not be good answers for either topic.

I hope you enjoy spending some time with this book. You may come away with a few ideas on how to best travel on this journey we call aging.

Did We Get Old?

I pulled into the parking lot, as I had done thousands of times before, and drove to my spot right in the middle. I don't park close to the school because, well, you know, that's where the geeks park. The good students, high achievers, the ones who get to school early to study or for some club meeting that's going to get them into the "right" college. And they did get into a good college.

Heaven forbid I park in the back. That's where the burnouts park. They pull in right before the bell rings and have one more smoke. Far enough away not to get caught. Of course, I thought they would end up in prison someday. They didn't. That was so judgmental of me, but that was part of high school. Am I right?

I'm a middle-of-the-parking-lot kinda guy. I stay out of trouble because that's what my Baptist parents taught me. I worked hard for my slightly better-than-average GPA, which would get me somewhere someday, although I had no idea where or when.

But today was different. I was not driving my high school car, a 1966 Dodge Coronet 440. White with a black vinyl top. A bench seat in the front to sit three and a back seat big enough for a party. And boy, did we party in that car. We always leave a special place in our hearts for our first(s).

My Cadillac A4 fits perfectly in my parking spot in the middle of the lot, with plenty of extra space around this much smaller car. No parties in this car. Something is much different, more than just the car. The school, the parking lot, and the football field look the same, but I have changed. I'm here for the homecoming game, part of my 45-year class reunion, so yes, I have changed.

I was the co-captain of the wrestling team and in the best shape of my life back in high school. Now I'm two inches shorter, yet 30 pounds heavier. How is that right? My thinning gray hair is much different than my Dad's bald dome. I guess I have my maternal grandfather to thank for what hair I have left. I do have a few extra dollars in my pocket, so I can upgrade my after-game meal and hangout spot. The place to go after the game during high school was Burger King, but we called it Whoppers. Meet you at Whoppers, we would say, when starting the plan for the night. The word Whopper was twice as big as Burger King on the sign, one of the many things about life I didn't understand at that age. But I'm much wiser now. They say we develop wisdom as we age, a result of collected experiences. Okay, I will take that and commit it to the truth, although some days I wonder.

I sat in my car, frozen in time, as memories flooded my head, so many memories. Damn the latch of a modern Caddy, so sleek and hidden in the lines of the door, hard to open, I thought. I wouldn't have had this problem with my old Dodge. That latch stuck out four inches and would always grab my winter coat pocket with every exit. But it wasn't the door latch keeping me in the car.

So many memories. Some are now enhanced over time, and some are gone forever, which may be a good thing.

I remember the first time I came into this very parking lot. My first day of school in my sophomore year. I was only 15. I sat in the backseat of a red Chrysler New Yorker. I was lucky to be driven to school by a senior, Norm, the older brother of my good friend Greg. Greg was in the front seat, and Dave, Bill, and I sat in the back. We had room for more.

The first day of high school is one of the most exciting and frightening days of your young life right? I had no idea what to expect. Back in ninth grade, we were the top dogs. Now we are at the bottom of the food chain and about to find out what that really means. I wanted to fit in—have friends, have fun, find a girlfriend, have success in sports, and, oh yes, good grades. Was that too much to ask on my first day of high school?

The parking lot proved to be an important part of the high school experience. A safe place where we celebrated wins, complained about teachers, and could relax. We talked about our favorite movies, *American Graffiti* and *The Godfather,* the original and best. We casually wondered about Watergate and worried about the war in Vietnam and the draft. We would crank the AM radios in the car to listen to some great music of so many genres: funk, rock, heavy metal, and disco. Let's not

9

forget the old-style country, which was depressing as hell. It seemed that every country star suffered from the same problems: the Chevy truck broke down, the wife left, and the dog ran away (the runaway dog more problematic than the wife leaving). But the classics —"Smoke on the Water," "Free Ride," "Goodbye Yellow Brick Road," and our class song, "Stairway to Heaven": When all are one, and one is all / To be a rock and not to roll / And she's buying a stairway to Heaven.

What the heck did that song even mean? We didn't care. Buried in the middle, there were two lines that struck me then and, in retrospect, may have been prophetic for many: Yes, there are two paths you can go by, but in the long run / There's still time to change the road you're on.

How many times did we change roads and, maybe, change again?

Today, I'm back in the lot. It has been 45 years, yet somehow I feel the same excitement and fright as I did on that first day of school. Will I fit in and find friends? Will I have fun? Funny how some things never change.

I was here for a football game. *Friday Night Lights* back at my old high school. Friday nights were some of the best times, with so many memories. I didn't play football, but many of my friends did, including my carpool buddies, Dave and Greg. Tonight's game would be different.

I got there early to ensure that I got my spot in the lot. There was no problem finding my friends; we kinda stuck out. Yes, Friday night lights launched the weekend of fun back then and now. Let's go!

It was wonderful to see people, some I hadn't seen since graduation. Some I didn't recognize. Our lives had changed, but within minutes we were all Edsel Ford Thunderbirds again. It's amazing how quickly you can catch up on 45 years of life. Just stick to the basics—family, career, travel, and health. We didn't try to solve the world's problems or our own. Leave that for another day.

Between conversations, I watched as the stands filled. The parents of the players filed in first and took their seats at the 50-yard line. Then right before kick-off, the students strolled in. That's where our story begins.

As I watched the kids, I mean students, I couldn't help but notice just how young they looked. Heck, we were not that young when we were in high school, I thought. Yes, we were. They did act the same, though. Some intensely watched the game and cheered. Others had no idea a game was even going on but were enjoying time with friends. The exact same as my group. All good.

By the fourth quarter, the outcome was clear. Short of a Tom Brady miracle times two, we were gonna lose. As it is in the fan world, the stands were starting to empty. The student section was the first to exit because it was Friday night—places to go: Burger King, I thought. No, probably some new place. A rather rowdy group walked by our section, looked up, and said, loud enough for all to hear, "Wow, look at all the old people." Wait, what did I just hear?

My first reaction was to look around to see who they could be talking about. No one in our group reacted to the comment, maybe out of good manners, or maybe, like me, they thought the kids were talking about someone else.

The game ended, and I made my way to my car in the middle of the parking lot. Well, at least we won our homecoming football game when I was a high school senior, I recalled. As if I was somehow getting back at the rude teenagers. In some small, silly way, I felt better, but for the first time in my life, I thought, Am I old?

What Is Old Anyway?

The next night was the reunion party. A fun affair at the local golf club in my hometown of Dearborn, Michigan, home of Henry Ford and Ford Motor Company. Growing up, it seemed that everyone's dad worked at "Fords" except mine. Yes, that also explains the name of my high school—Edsel Ford. (Edsel was Henry Ford's only child.)

I worked the room as hard as I could, in a good way, mind you. I wanted to take advantage of every minute of catching up, renewing old friendships, and making new ones. Some people I hadn't seen in years, and others I would never see again. But as I listened to the many stories about the roads people had been on, I couldn't stop thinking of the comment from the night before, "Look at all the old people."

Then an epiphany hit me while I was in the restroom, a place that men my age visit frequently. As I glanced in the mirror, I saw someone who looked vaguely familiar. He no longer looked like the 18-year-old co-captain of the wrestling team who enjoyed hanging out with friends and worked hard for his 3.4 GPA. This guy looked old, like he would be at a 45-year class reunion. That person was me.

* * *

If you have an hour to kill someday for some fun and frustration, google the phrase "How old is old?" In less than a second, 3,670,000,000 results will be displayed. Your results may vary, but you get my point. My search revealed over three billion websites with information about getting old and various related topics. I was curious to dive in for answers. Spoiler alert, there is no consensus regarding the definition of old.

What age is considered old you ask? The only definitive answer is: it depends. It depends on who you ask, when you ask, in what country, whether it's a biological or chronological question, and why you want to know.

We can't even agree on how to spell aging. Look it up, some spell it *ageing*. Here's a quick hint, both are considered acceptable. Ageing is commonly used in the United Kingdom—the proper English. We lazy Americans usually drop the mid-word *e*.

For me, and many of us, age is relative. My dad, whom I loved and respected dearly, was always old to me. He was bald, had a paunchy stomach, and wore glasses. His button-down shirt was always too long for his arms, his pants hiked up, and sometimes he wore a belt *and* suspenders. You can never be too careful, he thought. None of that made him old though. It was the simple fact that he was my dad, and all dads are old.

Oh no: I'm now the same age as my dad was then and likely older than some of the rude students' dads at the game (which is still no excuse). You can see where this is going, so I will stop.

I used the reunion event to conduct a brief survey, which turned out to be a bad idea. The single question was, Are you old? As expected, I got various answers, including the one classmate who promised never to speak to me again for asking such a mean question. In my nonscientific tally, most people would say no, or hell no. The focus group's average age was 63—you can decide if we were being honest with ourselves. This didn't help. The only conclusion that I could make was that "old is older than we are."

We need an answer. Some aging expert has to be able to define old and prove us right. Sixty-three isn't old . . . or maybe it is? Back to Google. Certainly, someone in those three billion will have an answer. Let's go.

What better place to start than with AARP (originally known as the American Association of Retired Persons, which proved too long for our memories, thus the shortening)? We can handle four letters.

According to its homepage, AARP is a US-based interest group focusing on issues for people over the age of 50. Fifty!? Well, that's not a good start. I thought this group was for old people. I ignored the membership solicitation for 10 years. Certainly, I was not old enough. I finally joined, thinking I would get free coffee somewhere, only to find out that McDonald's only gives a discount. Nevertheless, being a member doesn't make one old. Agreed? It's simply a discount card for special people. Side note, I signed my wife up as part of a family deal.

She was not happy about it. Her card is buried somewhere in her sock drawer. Screw the discounts. Moving on from my wife's feelings, AARP publishes quite a bit on aging. The organization must know the definition of old, right? Well, the answer isn't on AARP's homepage. I did find a study buried in the blog section. It was done in 2017 by U.S. Trust. The wealth-management specialists found that perceptions of old age vary widely among generations. Millennials, for example, say you are old when you turn 59. I never listen to Millennials, the generation of the participation trophy. Gen Xers hold a slightly more generous view saying old age begins at 65. At least that allows my class reunion peeps some breathing room. Boomers and the silent generation agree that you are not really old until you hit 73. You see the pattern here, right?

When asking the same groups at what age you reach the prime of your life, the answers are downright disheartening:

Generation	Prime Age
Millennials	36
Gen Xers	47
Boomers	50

Well, there you go. I passed downhill many years ago, but did I? This study only confirms one thing about old age: it depends on who you ask.

Research from John Shoven, the former Trione Director of the Stanford Institute for Economic Policy Research and the Charles R. Schwab Professor Emeritus of Economics at Stanford University, has a different look at the old. Let me stop right here and point out that he is an economics professor, not a science or medical professional, which begs the question regarding his slant on the topic. Let's read on; he is from Stanford, after all.

His take is how close to death will determine if you are old. Other than not knowing when death will occur for most of us, this seems to be an interesting point of view. Shoven suggests that a year is a fine measurement of time, but is not a good measure of age. Age he says, is strongly connected to health which is a key factor in determining conditional life expectancy. His conclusion is that age should be based on mortality risk or number of years you are expected to live. One part of the study was for the time range for the metrics provided, 1930 to 2020. The difference in age categories was staggering:

	1930	2020
Middle Age	44	61
Old	56	70
Very Old	65	77

It's important to note these numbers are for men. The ages for women were higher but equally different.

There are many reasons for the longevity revolution: access to clean water, sanitation, electricity, and improvements to health care, just to name a few. Maybe more interesting is what will "old" be in the future? According to David Sinclair, AO, PhD, professor in the Department of Genetics and codirector of the Paul F. Glenn Center for Biology of Aging Research at Harvard Medical School, there are people born today who will live to be 150 years old. Wow, I can't even imagine that. This discussion confirms our assumptions about old age. It depends on when you ask.

When you get to my age, you start visiting different websites than in the past. I will let you play with that line for a minute . . . welcome back. Seriously though, lives change, and our interests and needs do as well. One site I have been hanging around for obvious reasons is Social Security. How fun am I now? On this very interesting website, I stumbled across the Social Security Life Expectancy Calculator. I felt like I found the Holy Grail. This is it. The place that will tell me how long I have left, and I can back into the old age question. Let's go. Date of birth and gender is all they asked. Based on this "critical and extensive information," they are about to reveal to me the most important information in my lifetime. According to the US Social Security Administration, I'm expected to live to be 84.5 years old. Really? I will mark my calendar.

Okay, this is interesting. I need to bring you back from the excitement of the Social Security website. International Institute for Applied Systems Analysis demographers Sergei Scherbov (guest emeritus research scholar, Social Cohesion, Health, and Wellbeing [sic] Research Group, Population and Just Societies Program) and Warren Sanderson, guest research scholar, study aging and are evangelists about overturning the one-size-fits-all definition of old. Chronological age is only one indication of your prospective age. Scherbov's definition of old is not 60, 65, or 70. It's when your specific life expectancy is 15 years. That, he says, is when most people will start to exhibit signs of aging. Eureka. We have an answer. Wait—wait a minute. Just how do we know when our demise will occur? By this definition, I should have one foot in the grave since my hair turned gray 15 years ago.

While I do like the concept, the personal answer to old, it still begs the question, how do we realize the signs of aging? My gray hair aside, what signs are needed to mark the death spiral? Too nebulous and paranoid-leading for my liking. Let's move on.

I want someone, some expert, to give us an answer. A definitive answer to the question, how old is old. I like Scherbov's concept of age and its relationship to death, but the "when" is a bit sketchy. I need a death expert to fill in the details. Not Dr. Death, but a life insurance company. Yes, they are experts on the topic, which seems ironic for an industry that emphasizes the word "life." But in reality, they are betting the odds on death.

For example, Northwestern Mutual, whose main product is life insurance paid upon your death, has the advertising tagline, "You dream it. We'll help you live it." They are experts in determining when people are going to die. They have to be: their business proposition depends on it. So, yes, they are experts.

Northwestern Mutual likely has a sophisticated algorithm based on AI models that are predictors of when a person is going to die based on age, personal circumstances and lifestyle. I didn't call them to inquire, but I do remember the exhaustive pages of questions and the physical exam I took many years ago when I bought my policy. Experts! I can feel it, we are getting close.

On its website, Northwestern Mutual had a life span calculator that I found very interesting. By responding to a series of 14 questions, based on physical well-being and lifestyle, I will arrive at the age that Northwestern Mutual projects my demise. Can't wait.

Starting with my current age, height, and weight, the calculator starts me out at 80. A good start. Feeling good so far. Given my fortune of good health and relatively disciplined lifestyle, the calculator added years for the attributes of family history, blood pressure, stress (I may have fudged on this answer), exercise, diet, seat belt use, driving history, drinking (more fudging), smoking, drug use, and regular doctor visits. My updated projected death age is . . . drum roll . . . 98. I wanted 100 but am good with 98. Therefore, I should be old at 83. I had best get going on my bucket list.

Time for a workout break. I need to stay healthy to get to 98. See you back in an hour.

* * *

Okay, I'm back. Where were we? Oh yes, defining what is old. Let's go to the source for all things "true," Wikipedia. Don't laugh, I usually like Wiki content. It's often clear, concise, and even accurate. Let's see what it has to say on our topic. "Old age refers to ages nearing or surpassing the life expectancy of human beings." That falls in line with the theory of our friends Scherbov and Sanderson. Hold on, "surpassing life expectancy"? Wouldn't that just be dead, not old? Let's not pretend there is some overlap here. Moving on.

"Old age is not a definitive biological stage, as the chronological age denoted as old age varies culturally and historically." Yes, we know that, but it also depends on who you ask, when you ask, and why. We are getting ahead. Back to Wiki.

"Old age cannot be universally defined because it differs by context." YES. The United Nations considers old age to be 60 or older. NO. Most developed countries set an age range of 60 to 67 for when people in those respective countries become eligible for retirement and senior social service programs." And McDonald's senior discount for coffee is usually offered at age 55, although there is no company-wide written policy. Are we confused yet? Wait, more is coming.

Recently, gerontologists, the guys that should know (please note I use "guys" universally as men, women, or whatever, so I hope that's okay), have decided to subgroup definitions of old, just to make things less clear, more confusing, and maybe to piss off more old people, as you will see. The study set up the following groups: young old 60–69 (that's an oxymoron), middle old 70–79, very old 80–89, and super old 90+. Well, that clears things up.

Finally, one more source of wonderful information on old. (You should be happy I didn't recap all three billion sites.) A study was published by the *International Journal of Aging and Human Development* in July 2011. This must be good. It sounds topical, and it's international in scope, "Cultural Perspective on Aging and Well-Being: A Comparison of Aging in Japan and the United States."

The hypothesis was that older adults in Japan would rate aspects of well-being (growth, purpose, and positive relationships) more highly than adults in the States. To no one's surprise, the short answer was, yes, that's true. They found that people in Japan generally age better than those in America. There are many reasons for this, including lifestyle, diet, living arrangements, and emotional or social support. The most important aspect is that the attitude toward aging is different. Japanese concepts of aging are rooted in Buddhism, Confucian, and Taoist philosophical traditions. Old age is understood as a socially valuable part of life. The image of an older person as *sen-nin* (wise sage) is common in Japanese culture. And the pervasive Confucian norm of filial piety, in which children honor their parents, promotes the importance of continued respect and care for the elderly.

Aging in the United States occurs against a backdrop of cultural ideologies such as the Protestant work ethic and the American Dream, which define worth in terms of active engagement in work and responsibility to care for one's own actions and well-being. This provides an environment for economic growth, but shifts in aging and dependency are seen much more negatively in this context. I'm not suggesting one country is better than the other; however, in the discussion on aging, we have two very different environments.

Where does this leave us? Do we have an answer to our original question; at what age are you considered old? The clear answer is no. This does leave us with a good solution though. There is one and only one person—the expert, if you will, who can answer the question. That person is you. So, are you old?

So, How Long Do You Want to Live?

My wife accuses me of wanting to live forever. Given my spiritual belief, she may be right in a way. She thinks I don't ever want to die, like die in the flesh kinda die. She even went as far as introducing me to the concept of some type of cryogenic freezing for humans. WHAT?

Cryogenics, the prospect of immortality, involves the cooling of a recently deceased person to liquid nitrogen temperatures. The thought is to keep the body preserved until future science is able to repair or replace vital tissue (damaged parts, like replacing the brakes on your car when they go bad) and ultimately revive the patient.

Apparently, dying is a process rather than a single event, and a number of body tissues remain intact at the cellular level for a while, even after the heart stops beating. You do need to act fast though. Similar to raw chicken, you want to get that body in the freezer quickly so it doesn't go bad. Okay, that may not be the best analogy.

A lifetime member of a cryogenics facility pays a $1,250 deposit and then $28,000 to get frozen. Although some articles indicated a price north of $200,000 (must be the luxury version.) It's important to note that the price doesn't cover some extras or the cost to thaw and repair. YIKES. And prices are subject to change without notice.

I do find this very interesting, and it may be great for some people but not for me. It's possible that I have watched too many episodes of *The Walking Dead* series to be able to reconcile the concept of coming back to life. On the other hand, I wonder how many people 200 years ago would have thought the same about defibrillation and life support. Both cheat the dying process and extend life. Advances in science are amazing, and who knows, maybe in another 25 years, I will agree with my wife and decide to live forever. Cue the ominous music.

At the other extreme, my wife wants to go at 65. Go, as in move to Oregon and, you know, check out. (There are other states with forms of Oregon's Death with Dignity Act, and, of course, there are restrictions.) For years, this has been her plan. Makes you wonder if she watched *Thelma and Louise* too many times in high school or fell asleep listening to "My Generation" by The Who on her Sony Walkman, *I hope I die before I get old.*

Wait a minute. I'm over 65. Is this just a subliminal message to me, like a "there is the exit door" message? Let's say no for now and move on.

Back to my wife. Although my vision for aging is the polar opposite of hers, I understand where she's coming from. She has witnessed pain in the aging process. Her father suffered

24

from a lung disease, my mother was in a nursing home for years, and recently a close friend passed away after suffering from cancer. I get it. Nobody wants to go through that. She is not wrong. But is she right?

What about you? How old do you want to be? Moreover, do you even have a choice in the matter?

As it turns out, we have a significant choice in the matter. Yes, genetics play a role, but it's not as deterministic as you might think. Let's talk about genetics for a minute and get it out of the way. A widely held belief is that changes associated with aging are largely outside of our control. Many people think the way we grow old is genetically determined. That's only partially true and is a dangerous misconception because it can prevent people from taking actions that could help them age in a more positive way.

Aging is a complex process determined by a number of factors including genetics, environment, and a myriad of lifestyle choices. Many, many choices.

Since the mid-1990s, following the famous Danish Twins study, researchers have understood longevity to be only mildly heritable. The study was initiated to investigate the relative influence of genetic and environmental factors on the health of the elderly in different domains of health and functioning. I should note that if you have not heard of the study, no problem. It was "famous" in the world of science and genetic study. Yeh, I had not heard of it either until I did the research, but the article called it "famous". This spawned estimates that genetics only account for somewhere between 20 percent and 40 percent of one's longevity opportunity. Our health and longevity is not all about the luck of the family genes. Good news for all of us "regular" people.

If it's not just genetics, then what factors influence longevity? It seems that my advice to my kids when they were young was not too far off. Eat well, sleep well, and exercise in order to grow up big and strong, I told them. Often. With the implication that they'd live longer. This may be a bit simplified, but my point is that we have a significant opportunity to influence our own longevity. There are hundreds of books and articles that can guide us to success. Some are better than others, some are major quackery, but many are seriously helpful. One fun article written by Tanner Garrity is appropriately named "100 Ways to Live to 100: A Definitive Guide to Longevity Fitness." Spoiler alert: don't eat the hot dogs.

Do we want to live to be 100? If you ask my wife, she would say that's 35 years too long. It's not just how long we live it's how well we live. The quality of life is even more important. With that, I agree with her. I'm still not buying the out-at-65 thing since I passed that a few years back.

* * *

Roger Landry, MD, MPH, who trained at Tufts University School of Medicine and Harvard University School of Public Health, wrote a book called *Live Long, Die Short*. The title could be a mantra for how most of us want our aging journey to go.

Dr. Landry insists that how we age is up to us. His book provides the top 10 tips for a person to live a lifestyle that optimizes health and continuous learning, maintains social connections, and promotes a strong purpose in life. An "authentic lifestyle," he calls it. Wow, 10 tips versus the 100 found in the Garrity article seems far less complicated. But in the list of 100, you will find tips such as: eat dark chocolate, and drink red wine after five p.m. Maybe we can pick and choose between the two lists.

The good news is that these lists, and many more, can provide a wonderful roadmap for our aging journey. Not only how far we can go but the best way to enjoy the trip along the way.

However, let's remind ourselves not all are so lucky to have these lists and choices.

Set in the back corner of my class reunion party, back behind the last table, was a 22" x 28" poster board propped on an easel. It contained a list of fellow classmates who couldn't be with us that night because they had passed away. Fifty-six names were on the list, almost 10 percent of our class.

Dave, my carpool buddy, was on the list. Dave was the captain of the football team, very smart, well-liked, and had plans to be a doctor. Life took him down a different road in which he raised his family and had a successful career in health care management. His journey was cut short at the age of 60 after fighting cancer for a number of years.

At our age, we all have friends and family members who are no longer on their journey. May I suggest we take a moment to remember those we have lost? I will see you in the next conversation.

CONVERSATION 4

The Science of Aging

Welcome back. We are now going to chat about the "how" of living a longer, better life. To do that, we need to understand why we age. The science of aging. Warning- this conversation does get very "science-y."

I may be the last person who should be talking about the science of aging, or the science of anything, for that matter, as I'm not a scientist and don't remember much from my science classes where I worked hard to get my B grades. However, I do remember this story from my chemistry class in my senior year of high school. My teacher was an older gentleman. I was 17 at the time, so all of my teachers were older, but Mr. Smith (using a pseudonym to protect his identity) was, by all definitions, old.

One day, in his class, a group of us got feisty. Somehow, and I don't remember the how, we challenged our teacher to a push-up contest. If he could do 20 push-ups, he wins. Reminder, he was old. As he lowered himself to the floor, I started to have second thoughts, this may be a really bad idea. What if he hurts himself or worse? I mean, he is old. Before I could take action to put a stop to the mayhem, he was already up to 10 push-ups and going strong. He cranked out 20 as if doing warm-ups for wrestling practice. He won.

So what do I remember from chem? Not much. I can't tell you anything about the periodic table. I did learn, however, that old people are not as feeble as I thought. It's a more important life lesson than the periodic table, at least for me and plenty of people who are not chemists.

Tales of the fountain of youth are as old as time. I know this because I did pay attention in history class. Unlike science, history seemed more real to me. This stuff really happened with people and not just mice (this is foreshadowing; please keep reading).

First recounted in the writings of Herodotus in the fifth century BC, the fountain of youth legends became more prominent in the 16th century and involved Juan Ponce de Léon. As the first governor of Puerto Rico, he visited Florida in 1513, where legend suggests the Native Americans told him the fountain of youth was in Bimini.

Although Ponce de Léon never mentioned the fountain of youth in his writings, you can still find his statue in St. Augustine near a fountain of smelly sulfur water that many believe will heal your ills.

For those of us old enough to remember, Bimini was infamous for another politician's story. Senator Gary Hart chasing youth, in this case, a 29-year-old model, Donna Rice. Hart saw his political career sink in 1987 when a precarious picture— of him and Rice on the yacht appropriately named *Monkey*

Business—showed up in tabloids everywhere. The big scandal of the day may not even be news today. But back to science.

Much has happened in research since Ponce de Léon and even Gary Hart failed at finding keys to vital longevity. Maybe it took this long because aging was just a given. Death and taxes are inevitable. But now that people have found ways to minimize taxes, maybe next up is to delay the aging process.

A big break was a shift in mindset. Millions of dollars and research hours are spent on studying the origins of diseases, and for good reason. It's only when we know how they start that we can search for a cure. On a very personal note, I'm a huge fan of research in the medical field. My son is alive today because of the power of modern medicine. A story for a different book.

A conference at the Royal Society of London for Improving Natural Science took place May 10–11, 2010. This is the type of conference that goes on all the time without our knowledge or our interest. We would be bored. It is, however, the type of conference that we want to happen for the betterment of our future. Go, smart people.

Over the course of two days, nineteen presenting scientists built compelling cases that would challenge conventional wisdom about human health and disease. Summarizing the meeting was biogerontologist David Gems, who would reach the momentous singular conclusion that "aging was not an inevitable part of life but rather a disease process with a broad spectrum of pathological consequences." Simply put, aging is a disease. To anyone outside of the conference, it may have sounded like the seeds of a good science fiction film.

The Age of Adaline, in which Blake Lively doesn't age past 29, for instance. Or the classic *Brigadoon.* Nice to stay young, but the every-100-year thing might get old.

Let's recognize aging is a biological process, and if we study it like we do disease, we can understand the pathology, and that can lead to ways to manage or even cure it. Crazy thought, but let's get to the science of aging before we judge.

In 2013, Professor Carlos Lopez-Otin and his colleagues in the Department of Biochemistry and Molecular Biology at the Universidad de Oviedo (Spain) began to coalesce around a new theory that there is not a single cause of aging. In this view, aging and the diseases that come with it are a result of nine hallmarks:

- Genomic instability caused by DNA damage

- Attrition of the protective chromosomal end caps called telomeres

- Alterations to the epigenome controlling which genes are turned on or off

- Loss of healthy protein maintenance known as proteostasis

- Deregulated nutrient sensing caused by metabolic changes

- Mitochondrial dysfunction

- Accumulation of senescent zombie-like cells that inflame healthy cells

- Exhaustion of stem cells

- Altered intercellular communication and the production of inflammatory molecules

Researchers began to cautiously agree that if you address these hallmarks, you can slow down aging, forestall associated disease, and ultimately push back death. Oh, that's all. Well, let's get right to it. Just to explore the complications, let's go a bit deeper.

Although several hallmarks have been identified, cellular senescence, a cell fate that involves an essentially irreversible state of relative arrest induced by various types of cellular stress, has emerged as a prominent and fundamental aging mechanism that could be targeted to treat multiple diseases of aging.

Cells get old and consequently make us old. Sounds pretty straightforward. But wait, there's more. For my friends who took AP Biology and actually liked it, read on.

As highlighted in an article published in 2017 by *BioMedicine*, mounting evidence demonstrates that senescent cells accumulate in various tissues where they commonly develop a unique secretome of chemokines, cytokines, and extracellular matrix-degrading proteins, termed senescence-associated secretory phenotype (SASP), which can actively damage tissue, causing natural aging.

The senescent cells are characterized by phenotypic alterations, including upregulation of cell inhibitors p16INK4A (CDKN2A) and p21(CDKN1A), increased metabolic activity, resistance to apoptosis, telomere shortening, and decondensation of pericentromeric satellite DNA.

None of that's good. However, notice a key phrase buried in the middle of the scientific gobbledygook: "resistance to apoptosis." In other words, they won't go away. Let's engage our lab rat friends.

* * *

There is strong evidence in rodents that selective elimination of senescent cells, or blocking the detrimental effects of SASP, improves cardiovascular function and reduces frailty. Does anyone remember the 1972 movie *Ben*? It was the sequel to the 1971 movie *Willard*. Both plots had rats taking over cities. Okay, that may be a bit of an exaggeration, but here is my point. With all the scientific use of rodents, I have to wonder if the sequel to the sequel will have rats taking over the world, like *Super Rat*. Now back to science.

In subsequent studies involving old mice, two different senolytic strategies were used to kill senescent cells selectively. The studies demonstrated that each of the interventions improved bone mass and strength; however, before we rush to paint our protest signs Kill All Senescent Cells, we need to pause and ask what the downside is. Cellular senescence is not universally detrimental and can have beneficial biological functions like attracting immune cells to sites in need of tissue regeneration and healing. Dang, more work to be done.

In the meantime, let's harken back to that time in the movie theater with the credits rolling and Michael Jackson sweetly crooning: Ben, the two of us need look no more / We both found what we are looking for . . . .

Nope, we need to keep looking.

More Science-y Stuff

Let me again remind you that I'm neither a scientist nor a doctor. The following information was gathered from research from authoritative sources: the NIH, Mayo Clinic, and Cleveland Clinic; Harvard Medical School, Stanford University, Albert Einstein College of Medicine, and others.

At times, the information may suggest methods to slow or reverse the aging process. None of this should be tried without the supervision of your doctor. Because if there is one sure fact about aging, science, and medicine, it's that there is no single silver bullet. We are all built differently, and molecules, medicine, and even diets can affect each of us in unique ways.

Feel free to use this as your own jumping-off point to do your own research. There is plenty of information out there, and more research leads to new thoughts every day.

Read on if you want more of the technical information. (I recommend you don't bring this up at any party or family gathering, as most people don't care about this level of detail.)

Aging is characterized by a progressive loss of physiological integrity leading to impaired function and increased vulnerability that can lead to death. This deterioration is the primary risk factor for major human pathologies such as cancer, diabetes, cardiovascular disorder, and neurodegenerative diseases. Have I lost you yet based on this "pleasant" description? Follow me for more good news ahead.

Aging research has experienced an unprecedented advance in recent years, particularly with the discovery that the rate of aging can be controlled, to some extent, by genetic pathways and biological processes.

Carlos Lopez-Otin and colleagues proposed the original nine hallmarks of aging in 2013. In the 10 years since, the in-depth exploration of aging research has turned up additional hallmarks:

- Compromised autophagy: Age, oxidative stress, epigenetic factors, and mitochondrial dysfunction may decrease our cell's ability to perform autophagy, leading to the accumulation of damaged cells and accelerating aging. Additionally, the inhibition of this inner "healing" mechanism has been linked to Alzheimer's disease, type 2 diabetes, and cardiovascular disease.

- Microbiome disturbance: Dysbiosis, the disturbance of gut microbiome, can lead to negative health outcomes, increase systemic inflammation and speed up aging.

When the cooperation between our cells and the gut falters, the microbial community within the gut can become a source of infection, and can lead to age-related diseases, such as obesity, diabetes, allergies and even neurological disorders.

- Altered mechanical properties: Altered mechanical properties applies to both cells and extracellular milieu. From here the discussion gets extremely medical and complex so I have decided to skip it, but close the topic with the following happy note- The field of mechanobiology and its intersection with aging is very promising in terms of rejuvenation. That is all I need to know, but feel free to research if you want to know more.

- Splicing deregulation: This refers to the slicing process that constructs RNA from DNA, which is known to be impaired in older people. This is not the same as genomic instability, which refers to the DNA itself, nor is it the same as epigenetic alterations, which refers to the methylation of the DNA. Nope it is in fact its own hallmark.

- Inflammation: Chronic inflammation over time wreaks havoc on the body, which can speed the aging process, and contribute to many age-related disease.

The amalgamation of the old and new hallmarks may provide a more comprehensive explanation of aging and a way forward for research. The challenge is to dissect the interconnectedness between the hallmarks and their relative contribution to aging, with the final goal of identifying targets to improve human health and longevity. With that lead-in, let's provide an overview of the original nine hallmarks of aging.

- Genetic instability: A key common denominator of aging is the accumulation of genetic damage throughout life. This is especially relevant when DNA damage affects the functional competence of stem cells, compromising their role in tissue renewal.

- Telomere attrition: The progressive and cumulative loss of telomere-protective sequences from chromosome ends (kind of like the aglet at the end of your shoelace but way more important: you can replace shoelaces).

- Epigenetic alterations: Alterations affect all cells and tissue throughout life, including but not limited to DNA methyltransferases, histone acetylases, deacetylases, methylases, demethylases, and protein complexes implicated in chromatin remodeling. Unlike DNA mutations, epigenetic alterations are, at least theoretically, reversible, offering opportunities for antiaging treatments. Resveratrol has been extensively studied in relation to aging and its upregulation of SIRT1 activity and effects of energetic deficits in mitochondrial dysfunction. Collectively, the studies suggest that manipulating the epigenome holds promise for improving age-related pathologies and extending a healthy lifespan. Bottom line, drink more red wine, or so my wife would tell you.

- Loss of proteostasis: Aging and some age-related diseases are linked to impaired protein homeostasis of proteostasis. There are promising examples of genetic manipulations that improve proteostasis and delay aging. The compounds rapamycin and spermidine are both being studied.

- Deregulated nutrient-sensing: Current evidence strongly supports the idea that anabolic signaling accelerates aging, and decreased nutrient signaling extends longevity. Rapamycin, which mimics limited nutrient availability, has been shown to extend longevity in mice. Reminder, we are not mice.

- Mitochondrial dysfunction: Mitochondria have a profound impact on the aging process. As cells age, the efficiency of the respiratory chain tends to diminish, thus increasing electron leakage and reducing ATP (Adenosine triphosphate) generation. This, in turn, causes further mitochondrial deterioration and global cellular damage. The combination of increased damage and reduced turnover of mitochondria due to lower biogenesis and reduced clearance may contribute to the aging process.

  Exercise and intermittent fasting may improve health span through their capacity to avoid mitochondrial degeneration, possibly in part through the induction of autophagy, for which both activities constitute potential triggers. There is compelling evidence that compounds such as metformin and resveratrol are mild mitochondrial poisons that induce a low energy state characterized by increased AMP (Adenosine mono-phosphate) levels and activation of AMK (Adenosine monophosphate-activated protein kinase). Good stuff for worms, mice, and maybe mammals.

• Cellular senescence: Since the number of senescent cells increases with aging, it has been widely assumed that senescence contributes to aging. In young organisms, cellular senescence prevents the proliferation of damaged cells, thus protecting them from cancer and contributing to tissue homeostasis. In older organisms, the pervasive damage and the deficient clearance of senescent cells result in their accumulation, which leads to a number of deleterious effects on tissue homeostasis that contribute to aging. Senescent cells manifest dramatic alterations in their secretome, which are particularly enriched in pro-inflammatory cytokines, which contribute to aging.

• Stem cell exhaustion: The decline in the regenerative potential of tissues is one of the most obvious characteristics of aging. Hematopoiesis declines with age, resulting in diminished production of adaptive immune cells, a process called immunosenescence. Recent promising studies suggest that stem cell rejuvenation may reverse the aging phenotype at the organismal level. In particular, mTORC1 inhibition with rapamycin may postpone aging by improving proteostasis and affecting energy sensing, which may also improve stem cell function in the epidermis, the hematopoietic system, and the intestine.

- Altered intercellular communication: Beyond cell-autonomous alterations, aging also involves changes at the level of intercellular communication. Thus, neuro-hormonal signaling tends to be deregulated in aging as inflammatory reactions increase, immunosurveillance against pathogens and premalignant cells declines, and the composition of the pericellular and extracellular environment changes, thereby affecting the mechanical and functional properties of all tissues. There are several possibilities for restoring defective intercellular communication underlying the aging processes, including genetic, nutritional, or pharmacological interventions. Of special interest are the rejuvenation approaches based on the use of blood-borne systemic factors identified in parabiosis experiments. Given that the gut microbiome shapes the function of the host immune system and exerts systemic metabolic effects, it appears possible to extend life span by manipulating the composition and functionality of the intestinal bacterial ecosystem.

Are you still with me? That's a very high-level overview of the fourteen hallmarks of aging. Where does that leave us? For me and many others, I suspect, confused and longing for a simple explanation and a magic aging vaccine. Yep, but not happening. However, the science and medicine of aging have come a long way in the past 25 years, which is encouraging for the next 25 years. Our improved understanding of the underlying mechanisms of aging will facilitate further interventions and improvements for longevity and increased health span. There are things we can do now. Stay tuned.

CONVERSATION 5

Show Me the Money

Let's go back to the movie theme for a minute because this conversation is an extension of conversation 4.

"Show me the money!" Repeat that phrase many times, each time getting louder, with the last few so loud that you wake your neighbors.

Who doesn't remember that iconic phrase from the 1996 movie *Jerry Maguire*? Tom Cruise is trying to secure the contract of the prized Arizona Cardinal wide receiver Ron Tidwell, played by Cuba Gooding Jr. Gooding won the Academy Award for best supporting actor. The line is recorded by the American Film Institute as the 25th most memorable line from a movie. (The number one movie line, in case you're curious, goes all the way back to 1939, from *Gone with the Wind*. Defiantly spoken by Rhett Butler after Scarlett O'Hara asks, "Where shall I go? What shall I do?" Rhett responds, "Frankly, my dear, I don't give a damn."

To emphasize how much has changed in 27 years, the big money fictional Ron Tidwell was asking for was $10 million. Tyrek Hill, a real-life wide receiver, recently signed a four-year contract extension worth $120 million.

"Show me the money" is used as motivation in business deals every day. Because, as we all know, nothing happens without the money. That leads us to some very good news.

The world's billionaires are pouring money into the field of human longevity—and for good reason. First, the antiaging industry is expected to grow to over $64 billion by 2026, which is a 45 percent increase from 2020. Sounds like a good investment. Additionally, these folks are getting older, and what better use of their money than to extend their own lives? Remember the two givens in life—taxes and death. Since many of them have figured out the tax thing, why not tackle dying? Cryonics, anyone?

Investment dollars are being funneled into startup biotech companies engaged in developing a portfolio of solutions targeting specific biological mechanisms of aging. More about this later, and you will want details.

The (Scientific) Fountain of Youth

I'm wondering how many readers saw this conversation in the table of contents and skipped the first five conversations to get here. I mean, we all want the fountain of youth, the quick fix, right? Well, here we go, but I must warn you. You may be disappointed. Please note- ages included for affect, but may be different at the time you are reading this book.

A good place to start? Follow fame and fortune. Tom Brady, now age 46 and by some standards still the greatest of all time, evangelizes age-defying supplements, hydration powders, and pliability spheres. LeBron James, now age 38, young by most standards but old for a basketballer, is said to spend $1.5 million to keep in shape and stay on the court. Novak Djokovic, now age 36, hangs out in a pressurized egg to enrich his blood with oxygen and gives pep talks to glasses of water to purify them with positive thinking before he drinks them.

In the field of modern health science, these guys are amateurs compared to Bryan Johnson. Johnson, a 46-year-old centimillionaire who wants to be 18 again, has hired a team of 30 doctors and is spending millions to reverse engineer his body and brain.

You may be getting the point. The fountain of youth many of us are looking for is not a place but a process and can be very expensive and challenging, as you are about to see.

Johnson's routine starts at five a.m. with two dozen supplements and medicines, including lycopene for arteries and skin; turmeric to reduce inflammation; zinc to boost the immune system; a microdose of lithium for the brain; metformin to prevent polyps; and a green juice mixed with creatine, cocoa flavonoids, collagen peptides, and other goodies.

Lunch is equally exciting—a nutty pudding with almond milk, macadamia nuts, flaxseeds, half a Brazil nut, sunflower seeds, lecithin, cinnamon, cherries, blueberries, raspberries, and pomegranate juice. They lost me at cinnamon. I'm not a fan.

The exciting dinner finale includes a gray-brown goop composed of black lentils, broccoli, cauliflower, mushrooms, garlic, gingerroot, lime, cumin, apple cider vinegar, hempseeds, and olive oil. In total, 1,977 calories per day. No more, no less.

What does Johnson's typical day look like? Exercise, of course, and other advanced processes such as blasting his pelvic floor with electromagnetic pulses to improve muscle tone, as well as a daily application of seven different skin creams and laser therapy, and the occasional fat injections into his face to build fat scaffolding that produces a young person's fat cells. And then, there is daily testing of weight, BMI, waking body

48

temperature, blood glucose, heart rate variations, oxygen level, and others. Up to 10 tests for every organ. There is more, but you've got the idea.

After all that, I'm sure you are wondering about his results. As of January 2023, he has lowered his biological age by five years, has the heart of a 37-year-old, skin of a 28-year-old, and lung capacity and fitness of an 18-year-old with the bonus of overnight erections of a teenager. Mission accomplished.

My question is, is it worth it? It's not just a financial consideration. Imagine the time spent, the consumption of goop for dinner, etc. You can decide for yourself. For me, I was out at cinnamon.

There is good news found in there somewhere. We can exercise, sleep for eight hours, and eat broccoli. We can even step up our game with supplements, monitor our health, and regularly seeing our doctors. So really, the fountain of youth has been there all along, right in front of us. It was never a place or a fountain. It's more a process, a lifestyle. We get to decide just how far we want to take the process to stay youthful.

As I write this, I'm reminded of the 2008 movie *The Curious Case of Benjamin Button*. It's a unique story of Benjamin, who experiences an inverted life. Having been born an old man, he gets younger as the years progress. The saga unwinds a number of our expectations about aging. Please allow me to unwind your expectations. Nothing you have read will provide your sought-after fountain of youth, sorry. But the research is very promising, and some "miracles" are only a few years away from coming to market. Stay tuned and go eat some broccoli after you exercise, or whatever.

CONVERSATION 7

How Old Are We Really?

Sixty is the new 50. Well, no. That's what they say, but we learned our numbers back in grade school. We also learned enough math to know that 60 is, in fact, 10 more than 50. I knew math would come in handy one day. However, I do understand the spirit in which this little white lie originated.

Back to my reunion. Do you remember the old guy in the mirror, the one that was me? I did join my peers that night with a newfound curiosity on the topic of age. Some of the attendees looked older, and some were greeted with, "Oh, you haven't changed a bit since high school." A bit of a stretch, but, yes, some looked younger than others did. Just not fair.

The actions and movement of the crowd also intrigued me. Some sat and never moved except to get their food and an occasional drink from the bar. Others worked the room with precision, including the appropriate greeting, light conversation, and then moving on.

Then there were those who sounded . . . old. Please forgive the use of the word but let me clarify what I mean. Those with a feeling that much of their life was over, the good years were past, and now they were looking into a future of poor health, doctor visits, loneliness, and a drone of misery. Sadly and certainly, a few had that outlook on life.

The room was a perfect petri dish reflecting the factors of aging. We graduated from high school together, so we were basically the same chronological age. Yet we looked, acted, and felt different from each other. The years had been kind to some of us and not as kind to others. Genetics was a factor, but other factors like health, lifestyle, environmental factors, and attitude all played a role. We were the same age, but we were not.

Enter the concept of our biological age, stage left. Caution, we may not like this act as much as we think we do.

People age differently, thus the petri dish at my reunion. We were all the same chronological age, but inside we were different. Doctors have come to describe this as our biological age, how old our cells and tissue are based on physiological evidence. Our biological age determines our health, how we look and act, and ultimately our health span and mortality. From here, things get a bit science-y.

To assess one's biological age, scientists have been trying to agree on a standard set of aging biomarkers. Ideal biomarkers should outperform chronological age as determinants of disease and mortality. There are many to choose from, including telomere length, DNA Methylation, inflammaging markers, insulin-like growth factor, transcription biomarkers, gut dysbiosis, frailty indices, Klemera-Doubal method biological age, arterial stiffness, blood pressure (hey, we know this one), endothelial dysfunction, atherosclerosis, calcification, and more. I think we get the picture.

There is another problem: apparently, our organs don't always age at the same pace. Seriously? Please allow a brief car metaphor to illustrate the point. Our organ age depends on how we live, just as our car parts depend on how we drive. If we hit lots of bumps, our tires will deteriorate quickly, and windshield wipers will last forever in Arizona, although they may melt

For now, it seems the best biomarker we have to measure our biological age is called methylation. It indicates the interaction between our environment and the genome. Epigenetics cause changes in methylation across our genome, which modulates the activity of our genes. This has led scientists to coin the phrase *epigenetic clock* because it points us in the right direction to measure age. One such clock is the Horvath calculator, developed by Steven Horvath. It predicts our biological age based on DNA methylation (DNAmAge). The clock doesn't measure seconds, minutes or hours. For those of you who want to learn more, read on, others can skip a couple of paragraphs.

We are born with preset genetics outlined in our DNA. The genetic code is an instructional manual for everything inside our body (and will not be found in your glove box). Your DNA sequence doesn't significantly change over time. What does change is how certain genes are expressed. DNA methylation is a biochemical regulator of gene expression and occurs when a methyl group is either added or removed from a portion of our DNA sequence. There is an established correlation between DNA methylation and aging. The epigenetic clock aims to quantify aging based on DNA methylation levels. Got it?

Recently epigenetic clocks have become commercially available, often using saliva to evaluate DNA. However, there are many nuances to consider with the results. While epigenetic clocks have a high correlation with aging, it's still unclear of the accuracy or even agreed-upon interpretation of our biological age.

* * *

Just for fun, I engaged in two versions of an online test that was meant to interpret my biological age. Both asked a series of health and lifestyle questions you might expect in determining your physical age. One test determined my biological age to be seven years and five months younger than my chronological age; the other test, with fewer questions, predicted I was 15 years younger. I like that test better.

There are a number of challenges with the concept of biological age, but we can be assured that studies will continue as they could be key to understanding aging and how we can best deal with the process.

In the meantime, 60 is 60. But as comedian George Burns so intelligently said, "We can't stop getting older, but we don't have to be old."

CONVERSATION 8

The To-Do List

I grew up with a to-do list. I swear, the day I was born, my to-do list said to be born at 11:15 a.m.

I may have always known better than to rely on my faulty memory, an affliction that has followed me my entire life. If I wanted something done, it had to be on the list. That worked for me. As I neared the time of my retirement (semiretirement to start), I began to think that I wouldn't need to live my life off a list. It was such a feeling of freedom.

On my last day of full-time work, I decided to live the dream and not make a list. It was not the feeling of exhilaration that I thought it would be, but it was the plan, so I went with it.

On my first day of retirement, I slept in, but it was a Saturday, a day I'd normally sleep in. May I suggest that you retire on a Friday so you have the weekend to let things sink in? The following Monday feels so good.

I sat in my comfortable chair and drank my coffee. I had no list. This, I thought, would be a wonderful part of my future—freedom from the list. It wasn't.

It turned out to be an okay day, nothing special, nothing memorable. I felt no sense of accomplishment. I felt nothing, really. Is this how the rest of my life was going to feel? Nothing special?

No, that's not what I wanted. We work hard to get to this place. We can't retire to a life of nothing special. I thought back to the ever so wise words of a six-year-old boy, "This is the first best day ever." That's what I want. That's what we deserve. But to do this, I knew I needed a list. It just needed to be a different list.

My old to-do list had two sides. The left side was for work (my job), and the right was for personal tasks. Over the years, the right side has gone through a metamorphosis. No longer did I have the kids' track meets, all-day gymnastics meets, Friday night football games, Little League baseball games, or homecoming pictures. Those were replaced by dinners with friends, date nights with my wife, and whatever simple household tasks that my limited skills allowed me to do.

But now the left side, the work side, was blank. Wow, that got my attention. Such a freeing experience, leaving a lot of room to be populated. Nice.

What would my future to-do list look like? I struggled with the thought. When I sat down with the blank sheet of paper and the monumental task of planning my future, I came away empty. (You may use a Google doc or Notes app.)

For some people, and maybe you are one of them, the list was already filled. You knew exactly how you wanted to spend your golden years. Golden years—how does that make you feel? Anyway, your list may include golf, travel, time with family and friends, the usual stuff, and certainly great activities to add to the list.

For me, I just kept thinking, "First best day ever." I traveled a bit, had coffee with friends, and even started to play golf again. The usual stuff. Then the list revealed itself to me. The big change to my list was that it was no longer filled with things that I needed to do for others. The list presented the opportunity to do things I wanted to do for myself. This changed everything.

At first, the list started to populate somewhat magically. I changed the format so the top left was for places to go—errands if you will—and the top right was for the chores. A reactive approach. That worked for a while, but it did feel a bit mundane. Not "best day ever" material.

But then I added the power corner in the lower right section of my to-do list. And this was a game changer. This is where I listed my hopes and dreams. Things I always wanted to do but couldn't, didn't, or ran out of time for. Special travel, a new hobby to explore, and other bucket list things we are supposed to do before we die. This is where my book started.

Yep, my book started in the lower right corner of my to-do list. Just a dream that I didn't think would ever become a reality. I started to add small tasks in the upper right section, because it looked so much more manageable. I can't write a book, but I can write a chapter, I told myself. So I did. Then I wrote another. And after eighteen long months, I wrote half of the book. I wrote the last half in six months. It's amazing the motivation you get from seeing the finish line.

I love my to-do list. It still performs admirably to keep me on task. I still derive a sense of accomplishment by crossing things off my lists. Now if it's not on the list, it simply doesn't get done. My memory is not getting any better. Go figure. However, my list provides the inspiration and motivation to do more. It offers a list of potential activities, like writing a book, to make any day special. That list is limitless.

Not all days will be "first best day ever" days. But there is always a much better chance they will be if you have a plan. The power and freedom of the to-do list.

CONVERSATION 9

One Incredible Piece of Chocolate Candy

For 47 wonderful years of my life, I enjoyed a chocolate milk-shake every night before going to bed. Please don't hate me. This was a horrible idea for a host of reasons. It worked for me at the time.

But it wasn't about the shake. Oh, don't get me wrong: my shake was incredible. My world-famous, secret recipe shake. My kids got hooked on it as well; nice of me to share my bad health habits with my family. When their friends came over, they even asked for a world-famous chocolate shake.

No, it wasn't the chocolaty cold and refreshingly smooth combination of ingredients mixed by hand to just the perfect thickness that you could eat it with a spoon and still suck it through a straw. No, it wasn't that. It was because no matter how bad or good the day was, I was gonna have a shake. A reward, something to look forward to each and every day. It was one of the great pleasures of my life. Yes, every day was going to end well. Life was good.

I stopped the shake cold turkey when I turned 60. After consuming 16,732 shakes, give or take, I gave up this nightly ritual. It was hard, but it was the right thing to do.

I replaced the shake with a hot cup of green decaf tea. Nothing fancy, just the cheap stuff in a pouch. Tea is not the same as a shake, as I am sure you can imagine I tried the expensive fancy tea, but it didn't help. But now, I still drink green tea every night before bed.

This ritual has shown me the power of simple life rewards. I miss the shake, but now during my day, I do look forward to the tea.

When I semiretired from work, my wife announced she was retiring from cooking. Well, I like to eat, so I volunteered to take over the duties. So, yes, cooking. I went all in. Cooking and eating can be one of life's greatest pleasures. Just ask me. I live to eat, as horribly pedestrian as that sounds.

My research led me to develop my own cooking style. Something I call healthy and hearty, which basically means filling your plate with the fresh food I just made.

I shop on Monday at a small local store that gets a delivery of fresh fruits, vegetables, and meat that morning. I feel so European. The experience is pleasant. Close to the checkout is a display of locally made, individually wrapped candy. I buy one on every visit. The cashier knows not to put it in a bag. She hands it to me and smiles. The chocolate never makes it to the house, just a short five-minute drive from the store. But I savor every bite, so it takes the entire five minutes to consume this one-inch square piece of incredible chocolate candy. Just another one of life's simple pleasures.

Here's the good news. I noticed that these simple pleasures are easier to find as I age. Maybe it's because I have more time to discover them. Maybe it's because I have opened my mind to allow for more simple pleasures to feel like a reward.

Silly as it sounds, at times, I make it a game. Looking for rewards when I don't even need one. Did you ever think timing a green light could be a reward? Heck, I'm rarely in a hurry, but wow, I didn't have to stop at the light. It works for me.

Nothing big, just simple pleasures. The wrapper from the one piece of incredible chocolate gets thrown out on the way into the house. Nobody needs to know.

Someday I will start my nightly chocolate shakes again. It will be my reward for reaching my chronological age goal. In the meantime, I am looking forward to grocery shopping and my nightly green tea.

Who Am I Now?

Irecently got a call on my mobile phone, and I answered with my business voice because I get business calls on my mobile, as most of us do nowadays. It was a salesperson trying to sell me internet service for my company. Knowing that I had no interest in the conversation, I simply said, "I'm retired." He said congratulations and hung up in the middle of the word. No questions about how it was going or who he could follow up with. Nope, nada, nothing.

As I hung up the phone, actually an old term harkening to days gone by, we don't "hang up" phones anymore, but also not important to my story. As I pushed the End Call button on my phone, I had two very conflicting emotions. First, I was happy that I didn't waste any time on the call, but I also felt sad.

It was clear: as soon as I used the R-word to describe myself, it was almost as if I didn't exist, as if I had no value. Although he did say congrats as if to imply I just won something.

It reminded me of family game night back in the day. We'd have a wonderful time sitting around the table with snacks and maybe a 12-ounce bottle of Coke, playing games for hours. Do you remember the game Parcheesi? Parcheesi, introduced in 1867, is the American adaptation of the Indian board game Pachisi. The goal of the game is to roll the dice and move your four game pieces around the board to reach the middle or home. After you win, you sit there and watch as the others continue to play the game without you.

The R-word, retirement, is like that, or so it made me feel after the very short phone call—watching others play the game without you. But I don't want to be done. I want to keep playing.

So who am I? This is a question that we have been answering all of our lives. And as it turns out, the answer is a bit of a moving target.

There was a time when last names were linked to specific trade. The most popular surname in Germany is Müller, the word for miller, as in *I mill for a living*. In Slovakia, the most common last name is Varga, a word that means cobbler. In the United Kingdom, Australia, Canada, and the United States, it's Smith, as in blacksmith, silversmith, locksmith, or gunsmith. Yes, a whole lot of Smiths. These names date back to the Middle Ages when a person's job defined their identity and even their name.

Although our names are no longer an indication of our occupation, what we do for a living is still very much tied to our identity and often the first question we ask when we meet a person for the first time. It gives us a sense of who they are—their education, social status, political leanings, and whether they will be interesting or an engineer. (JK to all of my engineer friends out there.) Before we were married, my wife claimed she would never date a salesperson or a blond. News flash: I was both at one point in my life. But using a career as a conversation starter is not common in all parts of the world. The same question asked at a party in France is likely met with disdain, even considered vulgar, according to Frenchwoman Carole Gagliardi, manager of a New York art gallery.

Americans tend to tie their identity to their jobs, but for Europeans, employment's only one element of who they are. The bigger pieces tend to revolve around family, friends, religion, hobbies, and other interests. Americans live to work. Europeans work to live.

People in Japan tend to identify through family and family history. Denmark has a very relaxed attitude toward work, giving priority to leisure time, relationships, and hobbies. And the first conversation you might have in Bhutan may involve happiness, as they are the only country that puts its Gross National Happiness (GNH) score above GDP.

Now, when I meet people and they ask, "What do you do?" is my response simply to say I'm retired? That's what defines me now? It's actually not even an accurate answer. It doesn't explain what I do, it defines what I don't do. Are they then expecting a conversation of walks, reading, and pickleball? Or do they just cut to the chase and think, this person is old, retired, and adds no value to society and, therefore, none to me? Conversation over. Click.

Clay Routledge, PhD, professor of psychology at North Dakota State University, says, "While careers may be part of the picture, our jobs are only one puzzle piece in our lives. Ultimately, the solution is to diversify yourself." A person should have multiple elements that make up their identity, not like Sybil (remember the book from 1973- Sybil had 16 personalities?), but like puzzle pieces that fit together that show a bigger picture and tell a broader story. We are much bigger than just what we do or did for a living.

Let's take a minute to explore identity and discover why it's important.

Personal identity is how you see yourself, how you differ from others, and how and where you fit in socially. It could include your nationality, race, education, hobbies, interests, personality traits, or even your purpose in life. It's what makes you unique and reflects what's important to you. It's who you are.

Identity involves a sense of continuity, or feeling that you are the same person yesterday that you will be tomorrow, even when circumstances change. It's an accumulation of memories, goals, values, expectations, and beliefs.

And yes, it's important. Our identity reflects who we are and also provides direction for how we live life and who we become. It can provide clarity, purpose, and a deep sense of fulfillment. As Mahatma Gandhi once said, "Happiness is when what you think, what you say, and what you do are in harmony."

People who live a life true to their values and pursue meaningful goals live a happier life.

But there are times in our life, often times of major changes, when personal identity becomes blurred or even lost, in need of a reevaluation of some kind.

I remember standing in the high school parking lot on the last day of school my senior year. The sun was shining, the music was blasting was Alice Cooper's "Schools Out": "School's out forever." I did it. I was a high school graduate. It was a wonderful feeling, a feeling of accomplishment, the pressure was off: no more pencils / no more books / no more teacher's dirty looks.

It felt like I won. But now what? I knew who I was yesterday; tomorrow was not as clear.

The ancient Greek maxim "Know thyself" is inscribed in the pronaos (forecourt) of the Temple of Apollo at Delphi. Aristotle expounded the rule of conduct with the phrase, "Knowing ourselves is the beginning of all wisdom." The Greeks knew the power of identity. Although as I have journeyed through life, I have often found myself agreeing with Socrates, who said, "The one thing I know is that I know nothing."

"Seeds of our identity have been planted throughout our life as we discover our strengths, values, and how we fit into society," according to psychoanalyst Erik Erikson. "And, like a garden that changes over time, our identity grows and changes with new seeds that are planted."

I found that my identity has changed many times throughout my journey, as I'm sure yours did. I did find a new title after high school—struggling college student—and kept one lifelong seed as a University of Michigan Wolverine. Many other identities followed, some came and left, while others remained as part of who I am today: husband, father, friend, and lifelong learner.

Some that I left behind were DINK—double income, no kids (remember the 80s?), yuppie—young urban professional (also from the 80s), racquetball player, business owner, and vice president. This brings us back to the R-word. We don't have those job titles to fall back on.

In his book *Halftime*, Bob Buford suggests that wherever you are in life, consider it halftime, making game adjustments for the second half. Do you remember Super Bowl LI? Tom Brady and the Patriots went into halftime down 21–3 and came back to win 34–28 in overtime. Some pretty good halftime adjustments.

Not sure what adjustments to make? Author and futurist Buckminster Fuller asks the question designed for finding a second-half purpose, "What is it on this planet that needs doing, that I know something about, that I can help make better even in some small way?"

Retirement coach Dan Sullivan suggests reframing your mindset: think of your future without the encumbrances of the past.

Teresa Amabile, Baker Foundation Professor at Harvard Business School, offered this metaphor regarding her own retirement, "My career is like a moving train. At some point, I will get off, but the train keeps moving, now without me." It's frightening entering the unknown. But there are so many other trains that we can find with new experiences.

I was very tactical in my approach to retirement. I simply thought, how will I fill the 60 hours in my week that were once used for work and commuting? Simple and uninspired, to be sure, but it worked as a first step:

- Shop at the cool local market and cook healthy meals for five hours.

- Exercise for 15 hours. This includes walking the dog daily.

- Work on relationships for five hours. Breakfast, lunch, coffee, or calls.

- Learn and/or write for 15 hours.

- Work for 15 hours. Still consulting.

- Waste time for five hours. Because I can.

Last year I attended my daughter's graduation from Michigan State University. Her four years of matriculation were neither normal nor easy. COVID-19 changed everything, followed by the February 13 shooting on campus during her last semester. But she made it, and we couldn't be prouder. For now, she is a college graduate and will add the seed of being a MSU Spartan to her forever garden of identity.

The commencement speakers delivered messages of encouragement, exactly as you would expect. Thoughts of the future, reaching for your goals, respecting yourself, and staying healthy. Stay focused, but take risks and live big because life travels fast. I thought of my daughter as the speakers share their big hopes for her future. Hopes for health and happiness as she is facing this challenging and exciting life transition.

And then I thought, wait, is this message for me? I almost felt a bit guilty, stealing for myself a message that was clearly intended for the students. So I blocked the selfish thoughts from my mind until later. That evening I started to think of the messages that I heard that day: thoughts of managing transition, future, health, happiness, and reaching our goals. Our goals for the second half.

Is retirement like graduation from the best university in the world, the University of Life? I have certainly learned a great deal over the past 40 years. And as was said at my daughter's graduation "This is not the end, it's just a new beginning."

I'm thinking about taking a gap year or two. Actually, it's not a bad idea to do a little soul-searching—discovering, traveling, and trying new things.

Here's the beauty of retirement as it relates to our personal identity: I no longer have a title that tells me what to do for 60 hours per week. My kids have left the house, and although being a father will always be a permanently planted seed, my time requirements have been greatly reduced. I have the wisdom gained from 40 years of learning at U of L. And I have come to realize that of my four pawns in Parcheesi, only one, my career, has made it to the middle. I'm still in the game.

Now I have a new answer to the question, what do you do? My short answer is, I enjoyed a career in sales and marketing and am currently consulting and transitioning through retirement to become a lifelong learner focused on human health, happiness, and longevity. If I haven't lost them yet I might add, I love to travel, spend time with my wife, and live vicariously through my kids. Then I'd touch on to my current research, would you like to chat about your mitochondria or maybe methods to reduce your senescent cells?" Okay, they are gone.

What do you think, is my elevator pitch too much? I asked my wife and she said yes, too much. Her actual words were "You sound like a tool." Okay, I may need to tone it down just a bit.

During the retirement transition, maybe we need a little music. Will it be the Eagles' "Take It Easy" or Frank Sinatra's "The Best Is Yet to Come"? Both are good songs.

Is It Time for a Little Self-actualization?

Do you remember learning about Maslow's Hierarchy of Needs? Maybe in your second year of college in your favorite psych class? The one that was supposed to be fun and easy but turned out to be neither? The hierarchy was one of the few things I remembered from the class because it was so logical. However, I never fully understood what self-actualization meant. I felt at the time that I had a long life ahead of me. There was no need to worry about it. Well, maybe now is the time.

American psychologist Abraham Maslow introduced the concept in his 1943 paper "A Theory of Human Motivation." The theory is a classification system intended to reflect the universal needs of society, then proceed to more acquired emotions. While the theory is often shown as a pyramid, Maslow himself never represented it as such. The theory describes the pattern through which human needs and motivations generally move. According to the theory, for motivation to rise to the next stage, each prior stage must be satisfied.

The basic needs, classified as deficiency needs or D-needs, include physiological needs, safety, and love and belonging. Only when these basic needs are met can one move on to the higher-level needs of esteem and eventually self-actualization.

"What a man can be, he must be." This quote from Maslow forms the basis of the perceived need for self-actualization. Maslow describes this as the desire to accomplish everything one can, to become the most one can be. Individuals who are motivated to pursue this goal seek to understand how their needs, relationships, and sense of self are expressed through their behavior. Maslow also felt that it was important to "let go of beliefs that were limiting or had outlived their purpose."

It might be of interest to note that Maslow created his hierarchy working with Harry Harlow at the Henry Vilas Zoo Park—studying monkeys. No point to be made here, just an interesting distraction.

Self-actualization is said to be the realization of a person's potential, self-fulfillment, seeking personal growth, and peak experiences. This part of Maslow's research went beyond monkeys. He studied people whom he felt may have reached self-actualization by his definition. The elite list included Albert Einstein, Jane Addams, Eleanor Roosevelt, Abraham Lincoln, Thomas Jefferson, Mother Teresa, Aldous Huxley, Ludwig van Beethoven, and other highly accomplished people.

But this was not the only study that inspired the idea of self-actualization. In her documentary featuring Maslow, author and historian Jessica Grogan shows how Maslow further developed his theories by observing his grandchildren. He found self-actualization tendencies while watching his grand-children play; they demonstrated several key characteristics of self-actualization: spontaneity, acceptance, the freshness of appreciation, autonomy, and democratic orientation. A bit of a contrast in learning, don't you think?

Although we are all theoretically capable of self-actualization, most of us will never achieve it, or achieve it only to a limited degree. Maslow estimates that only 2 percent of the population would ever reach this state.

You may be thinking, why? Why spend time trying to strive for something that's attainable by a very few? Because, in Maslow's words, "It is critical to note that self-actualization is a continual process of becoming, rather than a perfect state one reaches." He adds, "Self-actualization is a matter of degree, and there are no perfect human beings." And the process can make us better. As we pursue a deeper sense of self and step into our potential, we may experience stronger relationships, better fulfillment, personal growth, and life satisfaction. The journey will make us better, and the journey is worth the effort. This might be one of those situations in life where you shoot for the stars and end up happy on the moon.

And, lean into this, Maslow believed that self-actualization is more suited for the elderly "because it requires wisdom and maturity acquired through the realities of life's lessons."

Stephen Jenkinson agrees. In his book *Come of Age: The Case for Elderhood in a Time of Trouble*, Jenkinson says, "Growing into elderhood can be like becoming self-actualized. Wise leaders act like self-actualized people." That would be us, my friends. It's our time!

And did you see that thing about peak experiences? Yeah, sounds like something we could use about now. Maslow believed self-actualization could be measured through the concept of peak experiences. This occurs when a person experiences the world totally for what it is, manifested with feelings of euphoria, joy, wonder, and often flow.

But how? How do we become self-actualized? It seems like the journey would need to include a trip to the top of the highest mountain to gain guidance from a spiritual guru, or Yoda. Great news ahead. While self-actualization may be an ongoing journey, it can be taken in small steps in our everyday life.

It starts with having a growth mindset, not being stuck in current habits. We will be looking to grow outside of our comfort zone. By taking on new challenges, or facing slight discomfort, we gain valuable insights about ourselves. This builds confidence and self-esteem. As each of us is unique, the trip toward self-actualization will lead us in different directions. But as Maslow will remind us, "A person is always becoming, never remains static." And this is key. We are not doing this for anyone else, we are doing this for ourselves because we can. Yoda, here we come.

To discover what can lead us toward self-actualization, who better to turn to than Maslow himself? In his book *The Farther Reaches of Human Nature*, Maslow describes eight behaviors that he suggests could lead to self-actualization, a pathway up the mountain, as I like to imagine:

1. Be present.
Experience fully, vividly, and selflessly, with full concentration and total absorption. Wow, have you ever done this?

I have not. I live so quickly, often multitasking, just scraping the surface of my surroundings. But it just seems life would be so much better when fully immersed. The sky would be bluer, clouds would be fluffier, birdsong would be sweeter, and the contour of my wife's leg even . . . oops, squirrel. Actually, a distraction or a fully absorbed appreciation of the beauty around me? I will let you decide. Either works for me. Imagine if we lived that way every day. I can feel myself making my way up the mountain.

2. Be aware of your choices.

Throughout the day, we are presented with choices. Maslow argued that we could classify most options as either progressive or regressive. Is the choice going to make me a better person or worse? Is it a safe choice or one that will take you out of your comfort zone and possibly lead to growth? Each choice affects our lives in some way. Our choice.

3. Get to know yourself.

"A human being is not a lump of clay or Plasticine," says Maslow. Who are we now and who do we want to be in the future? This gap may be the best opportunity for a path of growth, freedom, and self-actualization.

4. Be honest, most of the time.

There are times that diplomacy and politeness allow for a bit of mild cover-up. Maslow is clear in his suggestion that we should always be honest with ourselves, an important element in taking responsibility.

5. Don't worry about conformity.

Don't necessarily rely on the opinion of others. And at times, challenge your own paradigm. Is it time to get uncomfortable and grow?

6. Keep growing.

Self-actualization is not an end state. It's a continuous process that allows for growth and discovery throughout our lives.

7. Recognize peak experiences.

I find this to be intriguing and exhilarating. Who wouldn't want to live a life of peak experiences? Maslow describes them as moments of beauty and wonder. Everyone experiences them to some degree, but they can't be sought out. Instead, they must be recognized when they happen. However, you can create a situation where peak experiences are more likely to happen: doing new things, visiting new places, and meeting people in combination with a growth mindset.

8. Deal with psychopathology.

Part of becoming a better person means identifying and dealing with some of the least pleasant parts of yourself. Deal with them, and make the best of the rest. As a result of additional research, Maslow expanded the hierarchy from the original five steps to eight. Before reaching self-actualization, he added new steps:

Cognitive needs: knowledge and understanding, curiosity, exploration, and the need for meaning and predictability. I find myself stuck and enjoying this step in my life. Even as I write this book, my curiosity drives my hours of research (exploration) to fulfill my need to know and predict my aging journey. While I may not make it to the top, I look forward to living vicariously through others who do.

Aesthetic needs: the ability to appreciate the beauty within the world around us, on a day-to-day basis. According to Maslow, humans require beautiful imagery and pleasing experiences as we immerse ourselves in nature's splendor. Caution: peak experiences ahead!

And now there is a new top to the pyramid that Maslow himself never designed: transcendence. Yes, resting above self-actualization is a new stage, one that's motivated by values beyond our personal self, and feels very much like an intersection with our purpose in life.

Not everyone feels the logic of Maslow's hierarchy as I did in college—and still do. Critics suggest that the theory lacks a consideration toward individualism, cultural influences, and collectivism in the context of spirituality. And I understand the concern. But for me, and more important for many in the positive psych community, Maslow provided a firm foundation for understanding human behavior and motivation.

Now that we have established there is no need to actually climb a mountain for a spiritual awakening, may I share a story of an everyday experience that was self-actualized by a friend?

It's spring in Michigan, actually one of the three wonderful seasons that we enjoy. It's time for outdoor cleanup and planting. An everyday kind of chore. But not for my friend Tena. During a quick break from a Zoom work call, Tena described to me her plans for the weekend. An overnight trip to buy plants. For most of us, buying plants is a 90-minute chore. One that we check off our to-do list and move on to the next item on our list that we don't want to do.

But for Tena, this is no chore. This is a weekend experience that she has been looking forward to since last year. This two-hour drive is an annual event not just because the plants are beautiful and cheap; no, it's so much more than that. She and her friend go to walk the lovely grounds of the nursery, microbrew in hand, and look through the many varieties of plants to find the perfect mix for the yard and with hopes of discovering the perfect new variety for their signature look. They stop for lunch to enjoy a hand-tossed pizza—goat cheese and arugula—cooked over an open flame and maybe finish the day with a freshly made hand-dipped caramel apple topped with pecans.

For Tena, this was no chore. This, my friends, is a peak experience on life's road to self-actualization. A simple everyday chore that can lead to living your best first day ever. I love it. I will never do it, but I love it for Tena. We all have our own path.

If you're still looking for that first step on your road to self-actualization, take a little advice from Maslow: play with your grandchildren. It may be the perfect start for your journey. It's important to remember self-actualization (and now transcendence) is not the pursuit of perfection, quite the contrary. It's the acceptance of who you are, and being the best version of yourself. Hard stop.

CONVERSATION 12

What I Learned from Washing Dishes

Let me take you back to the 16-year-old me. Yes, it was a long time ago. At 16, I couldn't wait to get a job. Making money would provide the freedom I had longed for, maybe for a couple of years. I landed my first job as a dishwasher in a local restaurant.

My first night on the job, my first ever job, was horrible. My career path and life were ruined (dramatic effect). I will spare you the details only to say that when I got home, I told my parents that I was not going back. My dad had a different idea. And I went back the next day. This may have been one of the most important events in the short 16 years of my life, and it was important, as you will see.

The second night was not much better. Plus, I did the math and realized my six-hour shift had netted me about eight bucks. But I went back again.

Now it wasn't about the money. It was about success and winning. It was also because my dad told me to go back.

Okay, if I'm going to be here washing dishes, I'm going to make the best of it. So I turned dishwashing into a game. A game that I needed to win.

A little backstory to set up the rules of the game. Dirty dishes would be pushed down "the line," a conveyor belt made with metal wheels. I could hear when a tray of dirty dishes was coming. The conveyer was about 10 feet long, with four lines stacked on top of each other. On busy nights with 10 waitresses, they could easily fill all four lines. There was the constant noise of metal wheels turning. Trays were about 18 inches deep so the four lines gave us room for about 26 trays. Heaven forbid we ran out of room for trays.

If all four lines were full, waitresses would have to stack trays on the floor, and it would be a good indicator that soon we would run out of plates or maybe forks. None of this would be good. The entire success of the restaurant was on my shoulders—me—the dishwasher. Or so I told myself.

To win this game I set goals. The first goal was to never, ever, run out of line space. Not an easy thing to do, so I worked on ways to get faster—process improvement. This was in 1970 before Edwards Deming rolled out *kaizen*, the Japanese concept of continuous improvement, in US manufacturing.

As I got faster, I made the goals harder: no trays on the top line, then the top two lines needed to be empty, and eventually no more than three trays deep on the first line.

I loved the game, maybe love is a stretch, but the idea of setting goals, improving the process, and measuring success made the hours in the cold, miserable dish room bearable, more than bearable. It was a place where I could win.

Little did I know I had introduced the concept of flow into my life, a concept made famous in 1990 by author Mihaly Csikszentmihalyi in his book *Flow*. I had adapted what he refers to as an autotelic personality. I had turned constraints into opportunities. I made the job a game with variety, challenges, clear goals, and feedback. I had attained flow in the dish room.

So how does this story relate to you? You are likely not 16 and not working in a dish room. For now, remember my first lesson learned: flow. The second lesson learned from the dish room was purpose. If you remember somewhere back in my story, I mentioned the restaurant's success depended on my success in the dish room. Yeah, purpose. I worked hard because I allowed the thought to drive my purpose. True or not, it worked for me and it worked well.

And finally, I learned that effort and hard work can pay off. Simple. Something I saw my parents demonstrate my entire life. If something is worth doing, it demands your best effort.

I learned three very important life lessons in the dish room, three life lessons that helped guide much of my life. Lessons made possible by my dad. He said to go back, and I did.

We all have a dishwasher story. Teaching moments or life lessons make us grow or maybe even change our life. We can remember many things along the way.

Here is the beauty of this time in our life: Now we are armed with the memories and lessons we learned along the way. Things that made us who we are. And now is the time to use them as we look forward to all that life still has to offer. We are wiser, and life has so much more to give.

And, yes, maybe the most important thing for us to remember as we live our daily lives is that it's just a game. Let's have fun. Let's win.

The New Happy Hour

We have lived in one of the greatest times in human history. During our working years, we experienced three-martini lunches and the Happy Hour, a proper noun in my book. I, for one, was not a fan of martinis, but I do remember a great many ideas spawning from those lunches. And Happy Hour may have been one of the best therapies ever created for human happiness.

Yes, the Happy Hour. A chance to leave work a little early on a Tuesday night to enjoy alcohol at reduced prices. What a concept. Who cares that the drinks were weak and the appetizers were overpriced? It was a scheduled time for us to be happy.

There may be some irony to the name. I can recall many of the conversations being anything but happy, many involving complaining about work or life at home. I don't recall talking about health issues. That conversation was saved for breakfast with the guys, starting at age 60.

I'm also not sure why it was called Happy Hour; the happiness didn't usually start to kick in until the second hour or third round of drinks. Maybe it should have been called Therapy for Three Hours, a much more accurate name. We were getting our problems off our chests, and our friends would tell us what to do, while in actual therapy, the therapist would ask, how does that make you feel? It seems a bit backward.

It didn't matter because it worked for us at the time. Memories were made, and we lived to talk about it, even without Uber, although we really needed Uber.

Do bars still have Happy Hours now? I hate to ask such an uninformed question, but it provides a clear indication of where I am in life. Happy Hours at five p.m. are no longer on my radar. Five is now my dinner time.

May I propose a new version of the Happy Hour? One that isn't restricted by time or day of the week, or even location. And the new Happy Hour doesn't require the consumption of alcohol, although it could.

The new (and improved) Happy Hour is simply this: schedule a time each week to do something that you think will make you happy. Sounds lame and too easy? Well, that's the point; we want to make happiness easier. Please stay with me for a bit longer. I'm a big fan of happiness; please see the conversation about happiness in this book. With life as it is, sometimes we forget to be happy. "But...," you may be saying (and I can hear some saying), I read the conversation about happiness and it says you should not try to pursue happiness directly. I applaud you for the rebuttal, but read what I said in the last paragraph. You should do something you think makes you happy. Yes, happiness is not the end goal, it's simply the wonderful byproduct of the activity, thoughts, or circumstances that come our way. I suggest that you bring on those circumstances. Schedule the time, call it Happy Hour, Happy Time, Drunk with Friends, or whatever works. We all need to remind ourselves that life can be better when we are happy.

Let's acknowledge the fact that we are all different, circumstances are not the same for us all. Some of you may be thinking, I'm already happy. I don't need to be happier. Really? Is there a cap on too much happiness? Others may be dealing with situations that are causing some life struggles. May I humbly suggest that scheduling a Happy Hour may be just what you need at this time?

We are the greatest generation that lived with the Happy Hour. A concept that, in its original form, may just not be as relevant for us at this time. Maybe it's time to launch a new version—the Happier Hour 2.0. And I will still see you at five p.m. for the early bird specials.

CONVERSATION 14

We Should Live in the Blue Zones

Have you seen the movie *The Age of Adeline*? If not, you should. The 2015 romantic fantasy follows Adaline Bowman who stops aging after a near-death experience when she is 29. She stays 29. Kinda like some of us when asked about our age. "Oh, I'm 29 plus 39," which is to say I'm 68 without saying I'm 68. How clever.

The movie is actually well done and almost makes you feel this could happen, freezing your life at a certain age. As the storyline develops, we see subtle hints that not aging has its drawbacks. Can't think of any offhand, but they were there. Spoiler alert, in the end, she is able to get past this "curse" and starts to live a normal life in which she grows old and is happy. You have to see it to believe it.

As it turns out, the idea of "freezing" our age is not just in the movies. It may be a bit of a hyperbole, but please stay with me while I get through the exaggerated and awkward transition.

May I introduce you to the Blue Zones (not to be confused with *The Blue Lagoon,* the 1980 American coming-of-age survival film starring Brooke Shields and Christopher Atkins)?

The concept of Blue Zones is neither a movie nor a fantasy. They are very real. And they may remind you of stories about the fountain of youth.

The term Blue Zones grew out of demographic work done by Gianni Pes and Michel Poulain, published in 2004. A National Geographic expedition led by Dan Buettner took the work further to discover secrets of longevity in five places around the world where people live longer on average, and we find 10 times more centenarians than anywhere else in the world. Maybe the better news for us is that the people of the Blue Zones don't just live a long time; they live healthy, happy, and meaningful lives.

You may be asking, where are the Blue Zones, and when do we leave? In no particular order, they are-

- Sardinia, Italy

- Okinawa, Japan

- Nicoya Peninsula, Costa Rica

- Ikaria, Greece

- Loma Linda, USA

Dan and his team of demographers, scientists, and anthropologists were able to distill the evidence-based common denominators that account for the long lives and dubbed them the Power 9. Okay, that just took us back to thinking about fantasy movies again, but I promise this is true. Look it up.

To make it to 100, it seems that one must win the genetics lottery. However, studies have shown that the Power 9 can play a significant part in longevity. And, are you ready for the plot twist? They can help us common folk sitting in the audience. Yes, the Power 9 can slow aging even in us.

Now for the part you have been waiting for—the Power 9. Spoiler alert, you may be a bit disappointed; some of this stuff we already know, but we just need to keep after it.

Announcing the Power 9

1. Move naturally: The world's longest-living people don't go to the gym, pump iron, do Zumba, or run marathons. Instead, they live in environments that constantly nudge them to move without thinking about it. They grow gardens, walk to the grocery, and ride bikes to hang out with friends. Moving is just life. (Disappointed that this is so obvious? Well, hold on, we are not done being embarrassed.)

2. Have a purpose: The Okinawans call it *ikigai*, and the Nicoyans call it *plan de vida*. Both translate to "why we wake up in the morning." Knowing your sense of purpose can add years to your life and meaning to your day. This concept's big. I think I will dedicate a conversation to it.

3. Downshift: Stress leads to chronic inflammation, associated with disease. The Blue Zoners develop routines to shed stress, so much so that it's just part of their culture. Okinawans take a few minutes to remember their ancestors. Adventists read their Bible and pray. Ikarians take a nap. And Sardinians do Happy Hour with the world's healthiest wine made from the Cannonau grape. We Americans pay to go to yoga classes and download meditation apps. Hey, whatever works.

4. The 80 percent rule—*hara hachi bu*: The Okinawans' 2,500- year-old Confucian mantra, said before meals, reminds them to stop eating when their stomachs are 80 percent full. I may need to pray before my meal to ask God to let me know when my stomach is 80 percent full. But I do get the concept. Don't overeat.

5. Plant slant: Eat plants, and minimize meat. We knew this was coming.

6. Wine at five p.m.: We were hoping this was coming. Yes, people in the Blue Zones, except for the Adventists, drink alcohol moderately and regularly. Preferably the Sardinian Cannonau wine, which has up to three times the artery-scrubbing flavonoids as other wines.

7. Belong: All but five of the 263 centenarians interviewed belong to some faith-based community. The denomination didn't matter. Research shows that attending

faith-based services regularly can improve well-being, quality of life, and longevity by as much as 14 years.

8. Loved ones first: Centenarians put their family first. Old ones take care of young ones and in return, young ones take care of old ones. One centenarian from Okinawa described the feeling of holding her great-grandchild as "jumping into heaven."

9. Having the right tribe: The world's longest-living people are very social and choose friends who support healthy behaviors. Okinawans create at a young age *moais*—a group of five friends—that commit to each other for life.

Just how much healthier are these people? Well, residents of Nicoya, for example, spend just 15 percent of what Americans spend on health care but are more than twice as likely to reach a 90 in good health. In addition to the Power 9, they may have another secret; calcium- and magnesium-rich water that wards off heart disease and promotes strong bones.

The story of one Ikarian named Stamatis Moraitis brings it home for me. Stamatis moved to America when he was 22 to pursue the American dream. He was a painter, became successful, bought a house, got married, and had three kids. Maybe he had a yard with a picket fence and a dog, just to complete the dream.

At 66, Stamatis developed lung cancer. He moved back to his home in Ikaria. He started to breathe the air, drink the wine, and eat the local diet. After a few months, he planted a garden with no expectation of harvesting his vegetables. Thirty-seven years later he had a vineyard producing 200 liters of wine a year. When asked about his secret to living, he responded, "I just forgot to die."

***

This may be a fitting ending to this non-fairy tale story. News flash (at least it was in September of 2022). A bit of irony, the government of Italy is offering to pay people 15,000 euros to move to Sardinia (approximately $15,195 USD at the time the article was written.) There are some restrictions, of course: the money must be spent on buying and renovating a house and the house must be your primary residence. Sardinia is suffering from a shrinking population and weakening economy. Too many old people? Hey, it's never too late to live your dream.

CONVERSATION 15

The Science of Religion

Welcome to this conversation. I'm a bit surprised you are here, given the current state of religion in America. While 70 percent of people in the country say they are associated with a religion, only 47 percent are members of a church and less than 20 percent attend on a regular basis. I understand. Historically religion has had some issues. I mean there is the whole Crusades thing as well as other atrocities. Even today, we are divided by religion. Please don't get me started; I am not here to judge or preach.

As a matter of fact, this conversation is really not about religion. It's about longevity and happiness in aging. So don't leave the pew just yet, the singing is about to start.

First, I need to disclose my background as it relates to the topic because that's what's done in scientific journals to reveal any potential conflict of interest. And given my background, you may be looking for the exit sign. But I assure you I'm still committed to not being preachy. Hallelujah, oops, that just slipped out.

I was born and raised Southern Baptist, often going to church four to five times a week. Our friends and activities revolved around the church. In high school, I backed away from the church, not because I didn't believe but because I wanted to work a long shift on Sundays to make more money. Yikes.

When my kids were born, we felt church would be good for the family so off we went every Sunday. After trying a few, we ended up at a modern, rock and roll-style church with services held in a warehouse. As we drove up the first time, my daughter exclaimed, "This is not a church." She stopped going at the age of 16, like me.

But I have always been intrigued by the effect of spirituality on aging. Not because you always see old people at church, you do. But because many of the messages align with the lifestyle of longevity.

As it turns out the hunch was right. Do you remember the little mention of spirituality in the Blue Zone conversation? Yep, it's true. But maybe more impressive is the science I'm about to share. Yes, it's true. Religion and spirituality do, in fact, help with longevity and happiness as we age. Believe in the science of religion.

Much of the following information is gathered from comprehensive research published by the National Institutes of Health (NIH). Written by Harold G. Koenig, MD and psychiatrist, Duke University, this paper provides a comprehensive and concise review of research on religion and spirituality (R/S) and its effect on mental and physical health. (Notice the letters R/S. Science loves to abbreviate in papers. Religion and spirituality are elevated to science because they have their own letters.) This paper is based on a systematic review of original, data-based quantitative research published in peer-reviewed journals between 1872 and 2010. So yes, this is legit shit (oops, probably shouldn't be swearing as I write about religion).

A little history: religion, medicine, and health care have been connected since the beginning of recorded time. The first healers were often the spiritual leaders because, well, sickness was often thought of as punishment from the gods. This close association continued through the Middle Ages, and the practice came to the American colonies as common practice. Many of the first hospitals were built and managed by religious organizations.

The paper reviewed 1,200 quantitative studies from 1872 to 2000, and an additional 2,100 studies from 2000 to 2010. Eighty percent of the research involved mental health.

And as I suspected, and people in the Blue Zones confirm, R/S—religion and spirituality—do, in fact, have many positive effects on our mental and physical health. This shouldn't come as a surprise, but let's dive into some details.

- Well-being and/or happiness: 326 studies, and of those 256 (79 percent) found significant positive associations between R/S and well-being.

- Hope: 408 studies, and of those 297 (73 percent) found significant positive associations.

- Optimism: 32 studies, and of those 26 (81 percent) found significant positive associations.

- Meaning and purpose: 45 studies, and of those 42 (93 percent) found significant positive associations.

- Self-esteem: 69 studies, and of those 42 (61 percent) found significant positive associations It should be noted that many critics expected different results on the topic, given the religious emphasis on humility versus pride.

- Sense of control: 21 studies, and of those 13 (61 percent) found significant positive associations. This comes from believing that God is in control, and prayer can bring actions in life in line.

- Depression: 444 studies, and of those 272 (61 percent) found significant positive association. This was another topic where naysayers expected a different outcome, given many religions focus on sin and guilt.

- Suicide: 141 studies, and of those 106 (75 percent) found significant positive association of reduction of suicide.

- Anxiety: 299 studies, and of those 147 (49 percent) had less anxiety, 33 (11 percent) had more anxiety. Yes, this one is a little dicey. Anxiety and fear often spur people to seek comfort through religion. But as the old saying goes, "Religion comforts the afflicted and afflicts the comforted."

There were many, many more stats, but I think we get the point. But why, why does religion help with happiness and aging? It's a great question that may be obvious to some, but an interesting reminder for many of us.

R/S helps in many life situations. It provides resources for coping with stress that may increase a pattern of positive emotions. Those coping resources include

- Strong-held beliefs that give meaning to life circumstances and provide a sense of purpose;

- An optimistic worldview;

- A sense of control through God's answer to prayers;

- Promoting positive human characteristics such as honesty, forgiveness, patience, dependability, and gratefulness;

- An emphasis on love and compassion for others.

What about physical health and R/S? So glad you asked. When this section is done you may be asking me to save you a seat on Sunday or Saturday. Religious doctrines' influence on healthy behavior is often driven by the scripture found in 1 Corinthians 6:19–20, "Your bodies are the Temple of the Holy Spirit", therefore we should take care of it. Very strong motivation for keeping those New Year's resolutions to work out, eat healthily, stop smoking, and get the eight hours of sleep we need.

Let's talk specifically about the R/S effect on specific diseases:

- Coronary heart disease: 19 studies, and of those 12 (63 percent) found significant positive associations. Given the strong connection between psychosocial stressors and CHD, it's not surprising there is a positive influence with R/S.

- Hypertension: 63 studies, and of those 36 (57 percent) had significant positive responses. Religion has a way of lowering our blood pressure, although maybe not if you think you are "Hell-bound".

- Alzheimer's disease and dementia: 21 studies, and of those 10 (48 percent) found significant positive associations. Of note, some of the studies showed that a higher rate of dementia may have been tied to the fact that R/S individuals tend to have longer life spans.

- Immune function: 27 studies, and of those 15 (56 percent) found significant positive associations.

- Cancer: 29 studies, and of those16 (55 percent) had a lower risk of developing cancer or a better prognosis. Reminder, better health behaviors play a significant role, as does greater social support and less stress.

- Mortality: 121 studies, and of those 82 (68 percent) found that greater R/S predicted significantly greater longevity. The cumulative effects of R/S just make people live longer. Ironically, these are the people who tend to be okay with dying, given the belief of what's on the other side.

So, yes, going to church does seem to have a positive impact on our well-being and longevity. But before the recap, a note from Dr. Koenig, followed by my personal thoughts on faith.

An important point from Dr. Koenig: "Nowhere do I claim that supernatural mechanisms are responsible for the relationship between R/S and health. A relationship with science and a medical professional is highly recommended for all health matters."

As for me, my spirituality is certainly rooted in a long, interesting path. But my claim is that my relationship with God is based on logic. Yes, I'm prepared to explain this apparent conundrum, but I'm warning you, nobody is going to like it.

The explanation is simple. If having spiritual beliefs is going to help make me happy, healthy, and live longer, logically this is a no-brainer. Spending time in church every week and praying daily seems easier and maybe more effective than many other strategies that could lead to a better life.

I know, it sounds a little cold for something that should be such an important part of our lives. And I'm not saying it's not important, although I don't go to church five times a week as I did growing up. I do believe in much of the theology that I was taught, but many of my beliefs have evolved over the years.

I always thought that this way of thinking, of believing and living was good for me, not just as a passport to heaven, but good for me in the here and now. And as it turns out, science is on my side. Every night I say a short prayer. I thank God for all that he has given me: my family, friends, health, and happiness. I'm grateful. I then ask God to watch over my family, give them a good night's sleep, and keep them safe on the coming day. I learned a long time ago that God is bigger than the boogie man. I don't need to worry.

I have not mentioned much specifically about happiness in this chapter, although the physical and mental health benefits may have been enough to imply that happiness is an assured outcome.

But I still feel the need to introduce you to the happiest person in my life, my sister. I would like to point out that in the minds of many, including myself at times, she shouldn't be happy, at least on paper. She has many health concerns, watched her husband pass away from a very difficult cancer, and watched our dad die. She doesn't leave her house much because of her health.

Yet, she is happy, like very happy. I asked her why she was so happy. A leading question because I knew the answer. "Because of my relationship with the Lord. Someday I will be in heaven with Terry [her husband]. We will have dinner with Mom and Dad when I get there." And unlike me, she would be fine if that invitation for this weekend. So despite what I would think about happiness, she is, in fact, the happiest person I know. And I love her for it.

Back to science: A large volume of research shows that people who are more R/S tend to have better mental health and adapt quicker to health problems. The possible benefits to mental health and well-being have physiological consequences that have a positive impact on physical health, affect the risk of disease, influence response to treatment, and increase life span. There you have it- the science of religion.

See you on Sunday or Saturday.

CONVERSATION 16

The History of Aging

"And all the days that Adam lived were nine hundred and thirty years: and he died."
—*Genesis 5:5*

I would sit in Sunday school and listen to the stories of Adam and Eve, Noah, and Moses. Stories that helped to form the foundations of my spiritual belief system and never once did I ask myself, He lived to be 930? What? Noah lived to be 950 thanks to the boat. And Noah's grandfather, Methuselah, beat them all by living to be 969 years old, the oldest recorded age in the Bible.

Methuselah's name became synonymous with longevity. In 2010 biomedical gerontologist Aubrey de Grey, PhD, coined the term Methuselarity to refer a time when people won't die of age-related diseases.

But wait, let's back up 6,000 years or so. Were Adam, Noah, and Methuselah really that old? Moses, by the way, only made it to 120 and died young by Old Testament standards.

Well, I'm not the only one searching for explanations, and there are many to choose from. Some biblical literalists attempt to provide arguments to explain longevity including a better diet, and a water vapor canopy that covered the earth before the flood. That would help explain two biblical issues with one theory.

In 1907 the Catholic Church tried to solve the difficulty by declaring that the sacred writer is simply not using our version of a solar year. An easy explanation. Other biblical scholars think the ages are more symbolic and serve the function of linking the creation and the flood, ending the ten-generation sequence from Adam to Noah.

The Bible isn't the only place to find "extra" longevity claims. There are claims that the kings of Sumer lived for over 1,000 years, and Mesopotamians believed that living over 1,000 years made someone divine. Certainly makes sense to me.

Modern science would likely not agree with the stories of these super-agers reaching or approaching 1,000 years. Can you even imagine? But what social scientists would agree on is how people age, the attitude toward aging, and how cultural norms have been complex and varied for thousands of years.

* * *

Georges Minois wrote in his book the *History of Old Age: From Antiquity to the Renaissance*, "The ambiguity of old age has been with us since primitive society; it's both the source of wisdom and infirmity, experience and decrepitude, of prestige and suffering."

Minois begins his book with these words: "Old age: a term which generally arouses a shudder, two words loaded with anxiety, frailty, and sometimes anguish. Yet an imprecise term, whose meaning is still vague, its reality is difficult to perceive." Well, this sounds like a page-turner. But I have to admit, there is some truth in those depressing words.

As a human race, we have been dealing with aging, getting old, for thousands of years, I mean since Adam, for God's sake. And we still have not figured out how to do this well as a society. Why?

Let's explore this from a historic perspective and start with a little motivation from Prince. His 1984 hit song "Let's Go Crazy" seems appropriate: Dearly beloved / We are gathered here today / To get through this thing called life / . . . Let's go crazy.

In ancient times some strong, healthy people could live into their seventies, although most died before 50, probably as young as 35 in prehistoric societies. Those who were healthy were treated with respect, while the weak were considered a burden or even killed. The category for "old" was not applied as much to chronological age but to the ability to perform tasks and to contribute to society.

Civilizations from early Greece and Rome left art and writings providing a good portrait of the perception of aging. Few people reached "old," so elders were highly respected for wisdom, and councils of elders helped rule in society. However, respect for the elderly declined during the fifth century BC as the celebration of youth began to flourish. It's interesting to note that the first Olympic Games were in 776 BC. I think we can go ahead and connect those dots.

In one ancient story, Eos, the goddess of dawn, fell in love with a human named Tithonus. When he became old and weak, she turned him into a grasshopper and left. Okay then.

Throughout most of history, older people would be respected for their knowledge and wisdom, but that level of respect depends upon a number of factors. First was their health. Health care was not really a thing for most of history. In some cultures, people in poor health were viewed as a burden, were sometimes abused, left to die, killed, or expected to kill themselves.

The second factor was economics. When the crops were strong, the community could better care for the weak. Or, when older people had wealth (land, livestock, or money), they had more social influence and were treated with more respect. Some things in life haven't changed.

The third factor is the strength of the family. Early Eastern thought was largely influenced by Confucianism and other Eastern religions that valued family, so the elderly remained, and continue to remain, an important part of the hierarchy.

Let's fast forward to the early settlers, our founding fathers who built our country on religious freedoms. Certainly, they treated old people well. I mean, it's in the Bible- Psalm 71:9: "Do not cast me off in the time of old age; forsake not when my strength is spent."

The Puritans thought that old age was a gift from God, and as such, the elderly had much respect and power within society. Older Puritans owned much of the land, an important position in an agricultural society. Old People Rule, as the bumper sticker read on their wagons. And then the cars came.

During the 19th century, we saw a significant shift as the country moved from an agrarian to an industrial society. Value in society shifted from the farm to the factory and the need for large families declined.

I remember my dad describing his life while growing up on the farm. It was a hard life. And leaving aside the stale jokes of walking uphill both ways to school in three feet of snow, it wasn't a life that most young adults wanted to pursue. And so my dad, like many other young people, left for a job in the city at the age of 18.

But there were elements of farm life that he loved and brought into our family. Mealtime was great in our house. We all loved to eat, and we enjoyed each other's company as we shared stories from the day. Over time, we got busy, so the family meal was now relegated to a single day. Sunday was a special meal until that, too, became a victim of our busy individual lives.

As families broke apart for better jobs and opportunities, parents and older people were left behind, which was okay until it wasn't. People in the early 20th century lived longer because of improvements in sanitation and medicine but didn't have retirement savings, were not surrounded by hospitals full of specialists, and didn't have senior centers in which to hang out with their friends. The new factors of health, economics, and family structure led to entirely new problems of dealing with "old"—a perfect storm in a sense. And society was not ready. Why?

Old age is a recent phenomenon, historically speaking. In 1790, only 2 percent of the US population was over the age of 65. Today it's over 16.9 percent, and by 2030 there will be more people over the age of 80 than under the age of five. Did we not see this coming?

I grew up in a loving family, both parents worked, and money was tight. But there was always food on the table and a roof over my head. I do, however, remember my parents making reference to the poorhouse and how we needed to work hard to stay out of it. I really didn't think much of what the poorhouse could be, but I knew it didn't sound like a place I wanted to go. And it wasn't. A 1912 report from the Illinois State Commission described most poorhouses as "unfit to house animals."

During the transition from an agricultural society to an industrial one, older adults were left on the farms to work until they couldn't. Poverty in America became a significant problem. The poorhouses were the last resort—where older adults or the disabled would live, and work if they could, and, in turn, receive food and housing. In the 1930s, the United States was the only modern industrialized nation without a national system to care for the old.

Franklin D. Roosevelt signed the Social Security Act on August 14, 1935. Not everyone was eligible for assistance under the plan (a subject for a different book). The need for poorhouses declined, and they disappeared in the 1950s, only to be remembered metaphorically over the next few decades as motivation to work hard.

Then on July 14, 1965, Lyndon B. Johnson signed the Older Americans Act, which established services including meals, caregiver support, health services, transportation, job support, elder abuse prevention, and the Medicare program. And with this, America affirmed the nation's support and sense of responsibility for older adults. Yes, our government was in the business of caring for old people, but it was not popular for some at that time and still is not today. I believe that society should support older adults. And the government seems to be the organized entity to collect and distribute resources to those in need. I'm happy to see that our collective group of humans still considers this a priority. And I felt this way before I got old.

How did it happen that the care of the elderly went from care within the family to being institutionalized and in the care of strangers?

In the early twentieth century, 60 percent of people over 65 lived with their children. By 1960, that number dropped to 25 percent, and by 1975 the number fell below 15 percent. As economic conditions improved, children launched and were expected to move out of the house and pursue their dreams. The traditional multigenerational home grew less common. But all was not bad. The newly termed "empty nest" was often a lifestyle that older adults welcomed (as health and wealth allowed), and "the good life" of retirement took shape. Children and parents saw the separation as a new form of freedom. All was good until it wasn't.

Nursing homes were not developed to care for the aging population; they were a solution to a medical problem.

Hospital growth boomed as a result of Congress passing the Hill-Burton Act of 1946, which provided massive amounts of government funds to build hospitals. Nine thousand new medical facilities were built around the country.

In 1954 lawmakers provided funds for separate facilities for patients who needed an extended period of recovery. Most of these patients were older adults.

Nursing home care grew with the passage of Medicare and Medicaid programs in 1965. And by 1970, there were over 13,000 nursing homes taking care of patients with extended care needs, again most of them elderly. The explosive growth led to questions about the role of nursing homes. Is this where grandma should spend the last years of her life?

Enter the intermediate stop we call senior living communities. Call them communities, not facilities; call them residents, not patients, all to improve the living environment and avoid institutionalism.

Keren Brown Wilson, often considered the originator of assisted living, opened Park Place in southwest Portland, Oregon, in 1983. The idea was to create a place with more freedom and autonomy for a better life and add help as people need "assisted living." The place filled immediately and enjoyed a radical appeal. Today, the United States has 28,900 resident care communities with close to one million licensed beds, according to the National Center for Assisted Living. This number is growing daily.

The bad joke in the industry is, "Be nice to your children, they will be choosing your nursing home." I'm at an age where this joke has become a relevant conversation.

I spent some time late in my career in the senior living industry. I have seen the difficulties and benefits it has as a solution for older adults. Many of my friends have faced the difficult decision of what to do with their aging parents. It's not easy, speaking professionally and personally.

There you have it. Aging, getting old has existed since the beginning of human life. Has the process improved? Is it better to be old today than it was in the past? I suppose that depends on who you ask and when you ask them.

Maybe a better question might be, what will aging look like in the future?

The Future of Getting Old

Most of us will get old: that's our future. Please read on. "The first person to live to be 150 has already been born," claimed David Sinclair, PhD, professor of genetics at Harvard Medical School.

Longevity expert Dr. Aubrey de Grey, co-founder of the SENS Research Foundation in Mountain View, California, one-ups him to say that the first person to live to be 1,000 has already been born. This, to some, sounds like the beginning of a plot for the next science fiction movie.

I like a good futuristic movie or TV show. I grew up with Saturday morning cartoons, as many of us did. One of my favorites was *The Jetsons*. It first aired on September 23, 1962, on a Sunday night, opposite *Walt Disney's Wonderful World of Color*, but moved to Saturday mornings for the 1963–64 season because nobody can take down Disney.

The Jetsons was ahead of its time. It was the first show on ABC to be produced in color at a time when only 3 percent of Americans owned a color TV. But we watched it anyway in B&W. The Jetsons' daily life gave us a glimpse into our future. We saw flat screens, nutrition in a pill, treadmills, cleaning robots, video chats, and a version of a computer that got a virus. Future life looked pretty good and actually looks a lot like now.

But Hollywood was not always so kind with its predictions. Did you see *The Planet of the Apes*, the original and best, in 1968? Toward the end of the movie, Charlton Heston stumbles across the Statue of Liberty broken on the beach, a bit of a dystopian plot twist. Or what about *Soylent Green* and its climate catastrophes and overpopulation? I saw this the year I graduated from high school, in 1973, and thought, welcome to my future. Do you remember the secret ingredients for the food they ate? The movie was set in 2022—yikes. And who could forget *Wall-E*, the cute little robot left behind when the earth collapsed because of our misuse of the ecosystem? At least this takes place in 2805. Feeling a bit better.

But the movie that really got my attention was called *In Time*, released in 2011. The plot: "A future society where people have been engineered to stop aging at 25, and age becomes currency. The more you have, the longer you live. You work to earn more years, and lunch may cost you ninety minutes of your life." Of course, the rich had hundreds of years, whereas the poor lived from day to day, literally.But the concept of the movie is a significant reminder that our time on earth is limited.

The constant in every futuristic movie is that it starts with some premise of today's reality. Let's do that and see what our aging future looks like.

The premise—there will be a shit ton of old people in the world by the year 2050. This demographic shift that some call "the silver tsunami" started in the 1950s, the decade in which I was born. Kinda cool that I'm part of the giant wave.

Let's look at the data (worldwide numbers; US numbers follow a similar pattern) from the PEW Research Center. In 1950, there were 128.4 million people over the age of 65. That demographic grew to 530.5 million by 2010, a growth rate of 313 percent. We are expected to see 1.5 billion people over the age of 65 by the year 2050. Yep, almost triple. The percentage of the population for this age will shift from 5.1 percent in 1950 to 15.6 percent in 2050. And those, my friends, are the facts.

I'm thinking of two different plotlines for our futuristic movie, depending on your point of view of what our future could look like. The first movie, called *Ride the Wave,* tells the story of a wonderful life for older people as companies recognize the buying potential of such a large demographic. Fashion, entertainment, travel, and policy all cater to this fun-loving group that is out to make the last half of their lives as amazing as possible. Restaurants roll out healthy menus featuring foods from the Blue Zones, served only between four and six p.m., specially priced with a coupon. Health clubs pop up in every major city, featuring yoga (not the hot kind), tai chi, and pickleball courts as far as the eye can see. I want to see this movie. Heck, I want to star in it.

Then there is the other movie. This one is called *Grim Twilight: Society's Senior Struggle.* There will be a PG version called *Misery Loves Company* based on the same premise. This movie starts in the back rooms with politicians trying to figure out how to deal with the growing number of old people. The economic pressures are becoming too much for the social safety nets set up in the 1930s, when it was revealed that the life expectancy at that time was around 60. Nobody expected us to collect. And health care systems are full of old people with chronic diseases. Younger people are becoming angry about the drain on resources that are affecting their lives. This movie doesn't end well. Damn millennials, I knew we shouldn't have given them all participation trophies.

Two very different movie plots provide extremely different views of the future. And it's often said that the truth lies somewhere in the middle. We have seen elements of both movies already in our lifetime, so I think the movies have legitimacy. But what do the experts say? Preview, they have seen both movies.

The movie of the future will depend upon how we deal with the aging issues of today: health, housing, isolation, transportation, safety, financial concerns, caregiver shortages, elder abuse, and scams.

David Sinclair, who started our conversation with his big aging prediction, goes on to say, "The world's aging population will change everything, from cities, transportation, medicine, consumption, and even relationships between countries. The aging population will have an impact on the future like no other time in history. Everything will change."

The United Nations calls the aging population "a major success story," one that brings challenges and opportunities. Many factions of society will play a role in the outcome of this aging population story, and public policy is starting to catch up as countries around the world recognize the need to support this growing segment of their population.

Japan has one of the fastest growing older populations in the world. One third of their population is currently older than 65 and that percentage will reach 40 percent by 2050. This demographic shift is expected to strain their pension system and has already slowed the economy. They are seeing a decline in the working population of 40 percent. In 2000, Japan implemented a long-term care insurance program—thought to be one of the most comprehensive in the world. It even covers care models such as assisted living, home care, and assistance with grocery shopping. Tapping into Japan's historical design and manufacturing expertise has created an advanced age-care industry investing in care robots, health monitoring systems, and even regenerative cell therapies.

Singapore is another rapidly aging society with one of the highest life expectancies at 83 years. Its government has invested significantly in lifelong learning initiatives to boost society's human capital and to promote personal development and social integration. Universities support lifelong learning opportunities by offering relevant courses related to emerging skills.

For many social and economic reasons, countries are looking to raise the retirement age. China currently has one of the lowest retirement ages in the world: 60 for men, 55 for white-collar women, and 50 for women in factories. They are looking to raise the retirement age in the near future.

But raising the retirement age is not often popular, as seen in France. French President Emmanuel Macron used his executive powers in April 2023 to raise the retirement age from 62 to 64 and was met with massive strikes and days of riots in the streets. While raising the retirement age has tremendous benefits for the individual and society, doing so reminds me of the infamous football trick Lucy played on Charlie Brown. While I'm sure it's much more devastating to the prospective retiree, I want to divert this conversation to one of my favorite childhood characters—Charlie Brown. Are you with me?

Charlie Brown is one of the most recognized, loveable losers in our lifetime. When the character's creator, Charles M. Schulz, was asked why he characterized Charlie in this way, he responded, "Most people are acquainted with losing rather than winning."

Charlie Brown made his debut on May 30, 1948, in Schulz's comic strip called *Li'l Folks*. The gang changed to *Peanuts* on Oct 2, 1950. Charlie put on his famous zigzag polo on April 25, 1952, and has never taken it off.

Although never confirmed in the comic strip, it has been suggested that Charlie Brown was born on October 30, 1950. So yes, he is one of us, a baby boomer.

The first appearance of the infamous football gag was in the comic strip on November 14, 1951, but pulling the ball away on that day was Violet Gray. It's a role that would be filled by Lucy (van Pelt) in future occurrences.

Did anyone else notice that Charlie Brown never appeared to age a day in his life? Maybe this little trip down memory lane has us stumbling across a potential fountain of youth. No matter how bad his day was, Charlie Brown kept on kicking.

Okay, back to working longer. Once we get past the ball being moved, the benefits of working longer are numerous. On a personal level, working can be pivotal to one's financial, physical, and emotional well-being. We stay engaged in society, have a reason to wake up, and the extra money is a bonus.

Older workers help with economic growth and add to the tax base rather than subtracting from it. Companies benefit as older adults add diversity of thought and share knowledge with younger workers. Research from the Milken Institute Center for the Future of Aging found that older workers took fewer sick days, showed stronger problem-solving skills, and were more likely to be highly satisfied at work.

One emerging trend in the retirement process has been some form of phased retirement, a slow roll, so to speak. Rather than stopping completely, many people prefer to cut back hours. Currently, 19 percent of US companies offer some form of phased retirement, and that number is expected to increase. Speaking from experience, a phased retirement, often called semiretirement, can be a wonderful thing.

A key component for working longer is to stay healthy. A recent finding from the McKinsey Health Institute shows that "it's crucial for people to increase their health span. Innovations are needed globally to invest in the promotion of healthy aging, measurements of health, and proactive interventions to avoid and delay chronic disease."

Good news alert: this is happening. *Longevity Technology*, in April 2023, reported, "Companies behind the technologies to extend our health span, and compression of morbidity are in good health." Investment in 2022 reached $5.2 billion led by $3 billion invested by Jeff Bezos in Altos Labs. "Longevity investment is moving mainstream," according to the publication.

There are several companies focused on longevity research and development. Here are some of the top ones:

1. Google's Calico: Calico (California Life Company) is a research and development company created by Google to focus on combating aging and associated diseases.

2. Unity Biotechnology: Unity Biotechnology is focused on developing drugs to selectively eliminate senescent cells, which are believed to contribute to age-related diseases.

3. Human Longevity: Human Longevity is focused on using genomic analysis and machine learning to improve health outcomes and extend the human life span.

4. Insilico Medicine: Insilico Medicine is focused on developing AI-powered drug discovery platforms to identify compounds that can extend life span and treat age-related diseases.

5. BioAge Labs: BioAge Labs is developing therapies to target aging at the cellular level, with the aim of preventing age-related diseases and extending healthy life span.

6. AgeX Therapeutics: AgeX Therapeutics is focused on developing regenerative therapies to treat age-related diseases and improve health span.

7. Juvenescence: Juvenescence is a biotech company focused on developing therapies to slow down or reverse aging and promote healthy aging.

8. SENS Research Foundation: SENS Research Foundation is a nonprofit organization focused on developing regenerative therapies to repair and rejuvenate the body to extend a healthy life span.

These companies are at the forefront of longevity research and development, and they are working to address some of the biggest challenges associated with aging and age-related diseases.

It would appear that the fields of science and medicine are leading the charge in our future of aging, helping us to reach that increased health span we all long for. Well, most of us long for it.

But there are areas that still need improvement in health care. The traditional model of going to the doctor when we are sick needs to give way to a more proactive wellness approach. Early detection is key to almost all chronic health conditions. Treatment in the early stages of disease can make significant differences in outcomes.

Fountain Life, a health care company, claims to be "the future of health care" and suggests we become "the CEO of our health." Their model is "an innovative, fully integrated platform that aims to deliver best-in-class predictive, preventative, personalized, and data-driven health. A change from reactive to proactive, from amelioration to prevention." Basically, they want to help you—not get sick.

Okay, so we are going to work longer, live longer, and be healthier, but where are we going to live?

Is it me, or does there seem to be a senior living community being built on every corner of every town? So, you did notice, and it would be hard not to. According to the National Investment Center for Seniors Housing and Care, the number of senior living communities in the United States has grown from just a few hundred in the 1960s to over 28,000 in 2021. This growth is projected to continue well into the future.

The senior living industry may be building housing for Gen Z and the generation to follow. The silver tsunami is expected to crest in or around the year 2035 when the last of the boomers reach "old age." We will be hanging around for a while longer but our numbers will start to dwindle because, well, that's just what happens. We dwindle.

But I think this will be a perfect housing option for our future young adults. Think about it. It will be kinda like a college dorm, only way better. Have you been to some of these senior living places? You get your own apartment, onsite dining, areas to hang out, a game room, a theater, a workout facility, and more. Management may need to paint a bit, change the carpet, and the name of the place. But with a few changes these places will be good to go. And the inventory of potential buildings will be plentiful in about 30 years.

Having spent some time in the senior living industry, I can attest to the many positive things that can happen when older adults move into a senior living community. At the risk of sounding like an ad for my friends in the business: people start to eat better when food is available; loneliness gives way to new friend groups; brain health improves with all the new stimulation; safety is less of an issue; a feeling of peace of mind springs to life; and an overall better life is often the outcome.

However, it remains a fact that over 80 percent of older adults prefer to age in their homes, which can become a problem. But there are potential solutions to be explored.

Do you remember *The Golden Girls*? This American sitcom aired on NBC from September 14, 1985 to May 9, 1992. A total of 180 half-hour episodes spanning seven seasons. Four older women living together may be a perfect solution for the repurposed single-family home. As many said while watching the show, these women were ahead of their time.

Home sharing or cohousing will continue to be an option to meet the needs of circumstances. In Finland, it's common for younger adults who need affordable housing, often around colleges, to get cheap rent in exchange for taking care of the needs of an older adult. A number of apps and websites have seen success with this model such as Nesterly and SilverCrest.

And then, of course, there is the multigenerational family option. This is the favored choice for some countries and cultures and offers many benefits. And lest we forget, this is the way we lived in America for centuries. As is often the case, economics may drive this option from both sides. A recent trend finds college students returning to their family homes after graduation for financial reasons driven by student loans. Welcome home.

All these options would be supported by upgrading the house to make it safer for older adults. Building modifications would include making the house barrier-free. And, of course, technology would play an important role. We're not just talking about your grandmother's pendant so she no longer has to scream, "Help! I have fallen, and I can't get up."

Smart home technology could include devices to help control lights, doors, security, and a personal response system that now includes fall detection. Smart sensors placed around the house to monitor movement and activity are also a safe and nonintrusive way to monitor activity. And have you heard of the smart toilet seat? A 2020 winner of a National Academy of Medicine Healthy Longevity award, the toilet seat can collect actionable data about your health. Embedded sensors collect vital signs, including heart rate, blood oxygenation, and blood pressure. The information is sent to the internet's cloud, and your doctor receives notice of any unusual trends. What will they think of next? Oh yes, just wear the gadget on your wrist.

But let's address the most important detail in our story. The group that will have the biggest influence on the future of aging is not the government, it's not the private sector with an increased focus on hiring and retaining older workers, it's not even science working hard to keep us living long and healthy lives. No, the most important group that will influence our future is us, the old people. It will be up to us to accept the changes that we encounter. It will be up to us to remain active, healthy, and engaged members of society and to add value however and whenever we can. Yes, it's how we live and the choices we make that will determine our future in the aging journey and, in some way, the future of aging in our society. Challenge accepted.

For those of you who were expecting some great revelation about aging in the future, I apologize. The fact is that getting old can be pretty boring, as are the solutions to make our lives better. But just to make you feel better, let me share a delightful fictional story about aging. Do you remember our good friend

Charlie Brown? After making it big as a child actor, he left Hollywood and went into hiding somewhere in the Midwest, married Lucy, and had three kids. Charlie did finally show some signs of aging: he lost the one hair on his head. After laying low for many years, he started a little company selling books on the internet in July 1994. After searching for a name in the dictionary, he didn't make it out of the As, naming the company after the largest river in South America because it "sounded exotic" and was big. It was not the first name for his bookstore. The original name was actually Cadabra, but his lawyer suggested it sounded too much like cadaver, (this part of this story is actually true.) Did I mention that to hide his true identity, he changed his name to Jeff with a last name still starting with the letter B? Well, things went well for Charlie, now called Jeff. He recently showed his continued interest in the field of aging by making a three-billion-dollar investment. Yes, things worked out for the most bullied kid in the comics. You're a good man, Charlie Brown.

And one last fun fact, Charlie/Jeff liked the idea of being relentless, so much so that Jeff registered Relentless.com as a potential name for his online book store. And today, when you type it, you will be directed to Amazon.

Hey, but what about the 150-year-old who has been born? Her future is her problem. She may want to watch *The Hunger Games*.

CONVERSATION 18

When I Became a
65-Year-Old Orphan

This conversation is going to be a little different. No research studies, no science or medical terms, not even a little advice from a friend. This conversation is written from the heart.

It's a story about a parent's relationship with his children, told from my perspective as a father and as a son. I'm confident many will agree, a parent-child relationship may be the most complex, difficult, life-changing, demanding, and wonderful thing we may ever have in our life. I'm not selling the spousal relationship short, it just doesn't go through the metamorphosis that the parent-child one does. One that eventually flips as we get older.

I would also like to acknowledge that every relationship is different. This one is mine. I hope you can understand, relate, and even enjoy the story. The story ends with me as a 65-year-old orphan.

I grew up in a two-parent household, which was common in the 50s and 60s. My parents loved each other, as I could see through their actions and daily activities. And they loved me, told me they loved me, showed me they loved me, and supported me. But more than anything, they were there for me whenever I needed them. I knew that they had my back and that blanket of comfort was always with me.

And I loved them. But maybe my strongest emotion was respect. They were my parents. I'm not sure I fully understood their feeling of love, despite the fact it was all around me.

Then it came to me: When I became a father, I understood what parental love was, and the immense responsibility to provide a blanket of comfort for my family.

I remember the day we took our son home from the hospital. No longer surrounded by doctors and nurses, it was now up to us to care for this little helpless human. This was one of the most frightening days of my life. I was not prepared as I strapped him into his car seat. Did I do it right? Is it too tight? Too loose? What happens if we get into an accident? The drive was the longest hour of my life, at least up until that time. A drive made more precarious due to my precious cargo. We made it home safely. This was just the beginning.

As my kids were growing up, my parents were growing older. My relationship with my kids and my parents continued to evolve. I spent much more time with the kids, and my time spent with my parents seemed to be limited to holidays and birthdays. I wish I had done a better job with the balance.

My dad was able to take care of my mom in the last difficult years of her life in a nursing home. My dad would drive there every day, spend 12 hours with her, drive home, then go back again the next day. I called daily on my way home from work. The conversation was the same—food, weather, and how mom was. Do you need anything, Dad?

Then my mom passed. And things started to change. By this time, my dad was in an independent living senior community. My kids were active in high school, gaining their own independence. And my relationships at both ends were starting to tilt. I could see it coming but hoped it would be delayed. I wanted to hold on longer to be a part of my kids' lives and hoped my dad could remain caring for himself. It was only a matter of time until the dynamics shifted.

For a couple of years, I grocery shopped and brought my dad's groceries into his small apartment and put them away. Fruits and vegetables went in the fridge; his favorite Marie Callender's chicken pot pies went in the freezer. His cookies would remain on the counter, no reason to put them away. But one day it was different. Most of his old cookies were still in the package, and the fruit in the fridge had started to spoil. My dad needed me more.

For most of my early life, if I needed my parents, they were there for me. After I left home and even the last few years at home, I was self-sufficient and the need was minimal. On occasion, I would call home and ask for an opinion, not sure if it was for me or them. At times it seemed to help us both. But now the shift was complete. My dad needed me (and my siblings). It's the way life happens, and although my focus was on my dad, I couldn't help but think of my future.

The day came when my dad couldn't live on his own, even in a senior community. My sister graciously offered to have Dad live with her, which required a move to Wisconsin. The first time my dad would be living out of his home state of Michigan. By this time he didn't care where he lived.

My sister came to town with the plan of the two of us making the eight-hour drive to take Dad to Wisconsin. As I loaded Dad into the SUV, making sure his seat belt was neither too tight nor too loose, I was reminded of taking my son home from the hospital 19 years earlier. I had driven Dad many times before but this was different. Precious cargo onboard again. This trip didn't represent a hopeful, exciting new beginning. It was a cautious drive, taking nine hours instead of the usual eight. I slowed down to account for the tears.

My dad lived in Wisconsin for two years before he passed. He almost reached his 95th birthday. He had lost much of his mental and physical function. It was time.

I was with him when he passed, so I had the eight-hour drive back home to think and reminisce. Some sad thoughts and many great memories. As I was driving, it struck me that both of my parents were now gone. I was a 65-year-old orphan. I can't call my parents to talk about the weather or what they had eaten that day or who they had talked with on the phone. It struck me that no one in my life needed me anymore; it was an uncomfortable feeling.

It's tax season, and once again I did the kids' taxes. I don't think they need me to do it; it's more of a habit or convenience, or maybe it's just for me. Someday there will be a "real" need in our relationship. The switch will be for the last time in my life. Yes, I will need them. Good news, they both got a tax refund. I can rest easily.

The Happy Conversation

Are you happy? Like now? Ever? Always? And what exactly do I mean by "happy?" Why does happiness always seem to be just outside our grasp? And how does one get happy, anyway? Fair and important questions don't you think?

Over 2,000 years ago, Aristotle concluded that more than anything, men and women seek happiness. And today, some would argue, we still don't understand how to achieve that blessed condition—we have made no progress at all.

I beg to differ. I mean, come on, we sing about how to be happy. Just consider a few of the lyrics from Bobby McFerrin's Grammy-winning song from 1989, "Don't Worry, Be Happy." I love this song:

> . . . In every life we have some trouble
> But when you worry, you make it double
> Don't worry, be happy

. . . It will soon pass, whatever it is
Don't worry, be happy

The inspiration for the song came from a poster he saw from, Meher Baba a spiritual leader from India. And I must say, I think he has the right idea. So why am I talking about happiness in a conversation about aging? Because I think this is the absolute best time to be happy. And once again, science will back me up.

An 8-year longitudinal study published in July of 2013 in the Journals of Gerontology suggested that life satisfaction changes throughout our lifetime. Our satisfaction is at its lowest at age 21, starts to rise in our 50s, and peaks at 72. Yes, we are our happiest at 72, with only a slow decline into our 80s. No, no, no, some are saying, I was happy as a teenager, not a care in the world. First of all, really? No worries as a teen? Well, you will be delighted to know that, according to the study, our teen years were, in fact, our second happiest only to crash at 21, when the prospects of adulthood smashed us in the face. Yes, this little happy graph may be different for some, but, hey, science says we can be happy when we are old, and I'm a fan of science.

Jonathan Rauch, author of *The Happiness Curve*, presents a similar-looking graphic view of happiness as we age. In his book, he suggests that happiness is a U shape: we start out happy, our happiness does, in fact, dip in our middle years as we struggle with balancing a career and raising a family, then happiness starts to improve, which creates the right side of that U shape. He suggests that as we get older, the brain slowly changes to be less focused on ambition and more on connections to people.

Associate Professor Christina Bryant from the University of Melbourne provides an interesting rationale for why we are happier when we are older. Professor Bryant researches the psychology of aging and notes that not all people will feel affected by the happiness curve. Middle life can lead to great satisfaction as careers peak and our children move to adulthood. She goes on to say, and I like this part, "As we age through adulthood, positivity tends to increase, life satisfaction increases, and we experience less stress and regret. We develop cognitive abilities that enable us to deal with life better. Specifically, our capacity for more complex thinking keeps developing, which enables us to have a more nuanced view of life, which allows us to be happier and more content." Maybe this is us becoming wise. I look forward to that— someday.

But happiness is a misunderstood, illusive emotion. Dan Harris, the author of *10 Percent Happier*, a *New York Times* best seller, suggests that genuine happiness is more like "a fundamental "okayness", not a rainbow-barfing unicorn. We are not living in pixie dust forever." He goes on to say in his descriptive way, "Happiness does not mean we never get sad, that would be dysfunctional because life will give us reasons to be sad. Just ride the ups and downs like surfing a wave without drowning." Well, I don't surf and can't swim, so I'm not getting the comfort here.

Let's look at some advice from renowned happiness experts Desmond Tutu and the Dalai Lama. Their book, *The Book of Joy*, provides a host of wisdom regarding happiness and how to achieve a good life. It's an inspirational book to read.

The Dalai Lama says, "I believe that the purpose in life is to find happiness. The ultimate source of happiness is within us, simply a healthy body and a warm heart." Wow, this is big and we are off to a good start. We can find happiness within ourselves; I like where we are going with this.

He goes on to say, "What we want is not actually happiness, it is joy. Joy subsumes happiness, joy is far greater. Joy seems to blanket this entire emotional expanse." This may be more than a matter of semantics, but in the book, he makes a good case for joy. And it certainly works with the title.

Happiness is often a reaction to external stimuli. People are happy when they get a job, get married, or watch a good rom-com (not exactly on the same level, but you know what I mean.) This type of positive feeling can lead us to the hedonistic treadmill of pursuing pleasure for the sake of pleasure, a Greek school of thought that believed pleasure to be the ultimate goal. But once the external cause of pleasure is over, or the dopamine subsides, the happiness seems to dwindle.

Joy arises at a deeper level in your mind and tends to last longer, with a leftover effect of satisfaction. Okay, who wants to argue with the Dalai Lama? Joy can also be a way to approach the world—not a reaction, but a proactive attitude filled with kindness, compassion, and calmness.

This approach can change how we see the world. Happiness is often an inward feeling, how we are affected, and how we feel and act. Joy provides a wider perspective—zoom out, if you will—and moves beyond limited self-awareness and self-interest, reframing our views with a more positive perspective. Sort of a long view on life. Wow, I don't know about you, but I'm feeling a bit of a spiritual awakening listening to the words of the Dalai Lama.

Before we leave his wisdom, I need to share with you his eight pillars of joy. The way we can live a life of joyfulness (be happy for us common folk).

I'm just providing the list of words, most self-explanatory. But for deeper details, again I would highly recommend reading *The Book of Joy*.

1. Perspective

2. Humility

3. Humor

4. Acceptance

5. Forgiveness

6. Gratitude

7. Compassion

8. Generosity

Allow me to leave the Dalai Lama section with one of my favorite quotes from the book. It reflects the first pillar, perspective. So simple. So profound. So life changing: "Why be unhappy about something if it can be remedied? And everything can be remedied."

* * *

133

When UC Berkeley released its 2022 study from The Greater Good Science Center it showed how we regular people can live happier, more meaningful lives. There are four things, and maybe not what we expect. But, hey, this is from Berkeley (smart, forward-thinking people).

1. Savoring everyday pleasures can give life more meaning. Simply paying attention to small joys can provide a path toward purpose and meaning.

   I did really enjoy the blue sky today, something we get very little of in the winter here in Michigan.

2. To achieve more, chase discomfort, not success. Growing is often uncomfortable, but embracing discomfort can be motivating.

3. We underestimate the power of kindness. One study showed how kindness affects our health by reducing gene activation tied to inflammation.

4. Awe helps us feel connected. That feeling of profound pleasure in smallness by looking up at the sky.

Nice thoughts but there has to be more.

Laurie Santos, PhD, may hold the record for making people happier. Professor Santos teaches the most popular class in the history of Yale University, "The Science of Well-Being." Students can take the course in person on campus, and it's available through Coursera, where millions of people have taken the class, including me. She also has a podcast called *The*

Happiness Lab, which has been downloaded over 90 million times since launching in 2019.

The purpose of the class and the topic of many of the podcasts is to discover a happier, more fulfilling life with less stress. "Knowing what to do is only half the battle," she says in her class. "Knowing is not enough, one must change habits. We can change our life by changing our habits. Changes to our lifestyle can put us in a place that allows for happiness and moments of joy. The key is to take small steps toward happiness based on science. If you want to change your life, you need to change the way you live."

There are actually so many things I like about this approach. First, it's based on science. Throughout the class, she will suggest a practice we should include in our lives and then provide mountains of scientific evidence as to why it works. I love science. My science teachers would be so proud. I appreciate that this is a proactive approach. So often we find happiness is a result of something—an external event—that causes us to be happy. It's a reaction. And once the activity goes away, our happiness goes with it. Dr. Santos's teachings provide a more proactive approach with healthy lifestyle changes that allow for happiness to find us more often, with lingering positive feelings.

And finally, well-being: the state of being comfortable, healthy, and happy. Well-being is the process of managing all the dimensions of our life to achieve the ultimate goal of a good life (happiness). This can set us up to find happiness or for happiness to find us, by being in the right place with the right mindset. Happiness itself is not a place, but a byproduct of the experiences we have along our journey. This sounds like a great way to approach life. Or maybe it should be a bumper sticker.

Here are some of the lifestyle activities that Dr. Santos recommends that lead to a life of well-being:

1. Connect with people. As the earlier Harvard study showed, our relationships often are the most important element leading to our happiness.

2. Practice gratitude. I am thankful for this.

3. Savor life. Love the little moments.

4. Avoid social comparison. This has "let go of social media" written all over it. And, in fact, it's a recommendation.

5. Be healthy. Sleep, exercise, and eat well. There is a strong connection between physical health, mental health, well-being, and, specifically, happiness.

6. Invest in experiences rather than stuff. Spend your money and time on a trip, a book club, or time with family and friends. Stuff doesn't bring joy in the long term.

7. Understand that happiness is a journey and not a place. We joke about being in our "happy place," and that's a nice metaphor and, yes, being on that special vacation can lead to happiness (see above). But nobody is happy all the time. Happiness is a wonderful byproduct of living life well.

8. Seek Kindness. No explanation is needed.

9. Meditate. Calm your thoughts. I must admit I'm not into meditation. I have tried, and either I fall asleep or start thinking about the three things I need to do right after meditation. For those of you who have mastered your mind, I applaud you. Maybe I will keep trying, and someday we can hum together (sarcastic meditation joke).

10. Reduce decision fatigue. What? Too many choices can be exhausting and overwhelming. So yes, clean your closet, say no, narrow your choices, and see how you can make life easier, and easier can be an important component of well-being.

All good advice.

Maybe we know more about happiness than Socrates gave us credit for. Stoic sages, men like Marcus Aurelius and Seneca, marveled at the sublime mystery of being alive and offered advice for leading a life marked by real joy.

Other Hellenic philosophers, like Plato and Aristotle, speculated on ethereal questions: Is there life after death? Why do we exist? What is the meaning of life? The Stoics, meanwhile, grappled with the question of what makes a good life. While the answers were multifaceted, most agreed on the importance of cultivating eudaemonia, inner peace that could weather all vicissitudes (their words, not mine).

The Stoics advocated a simple yet powerful technique called negative visualization. With negative visualization, you imagine life without the things and people you currently have, and then remind yourself you still have them—your home, your health, your family, and your friends. In this way, they fostered gratitude and lived with the mantra that life could be worse, which might seem cold but can take the sting out of life's disappointments.

Maybe we've had the keys to happiness all along. But, like our struggles today, it's just difficult to find them.

Let me leave you with the wisdom of happiness from another contemporary singer-songwriter, Pharrell Williams. His hit "Happy," featured in the soundtrack of *Despicable Me 2*, was number one in the United States and 23 countries and the 8th highest selling single of all time in the United Kingdom. Which just goes to prove that people wanna be happy.

Sing along with me:

> Clap along if you feel like happiness is the truth
> Clap along if you know what happiness is to you
> Clap along if you feel like that's what you wanna do
> . . . Because I'm Happy

Guys With(out) Friends

This is a problem that's somewhat unique to guys, but ladies, please stay with me, we need you, as you will soon see. Men have fewer friends as we get older; it's a fact that we just ignore because, well, we don't think it's a problem.

I have friends, I thought, until I thought about it. As it turns out, most of my friends are the husbands of my wife's friends. We see them when the couples get together, and that works for me. But does it?

As it turns out, friends and relationships are very important for our well-being. For 84 years and counting, Harvard has been conducting the longest known study regarding happiness. The study, starting in 1938, tracked the lives of 724 men and then extended to their families, asking thousands of questions and taking hundreds of measurements to find out what really keeps people happy. One crucial factor stands out. It's not career achievement, exercise, or a healthy diet, although all are contributors. But one thing continuously demonstrates a broad and enduring source of happiness—good relationships.

Robert Waldinger, MD clinical professor of psychiatry at Harvard Medical School, is the study's fourth director. He coauthored *The Good Life: Lessons from the World's Longest Scientific Study.* There he states, "If we had to take all 84 years of the Harvard study and boil it down into a single principle for living it would be this: good relationships keep us healthier and happier (and lead to a longer life)." Period. A finding that has been supported by many other studies.

Growing up, we heard happiness advice that would stay with us all day with Jimmy Soul's number one hit song from 1963, "If You Wanna Be Happy."

> If you wanna be happy for the rest of your life
> Never make a pretty woman your wife
> So for my personal point of view
> Get an ugly girl to marry you

As it turns out, it's not her looks that matter; it's your relationship that makes you happy. Not sure how many of you followed his advice, but in my personal point of view, I'm happy I didn't. By the way, sorry for invading your headspace; the song will be in there all day.

* * *

Making and retaining friends as an adult is hard. Sometimes I don't need research to provide such obvious truths. This would be one of those times. Less than half of men surveyed report being satisfied with their relationships, and only one in five said they receive emotional support from a friend, compared to four in ten for women, according to a 2021 survey from the Survey Center on American Life. Yep, it's a guy problem.

The falling off of relationships for males begins around middle and late adolescence and grows starker into adulthood, according to Judy Yi-Chung Chu, who lectures on boys' psychological development at Stanford University. More smart people telling me stuff I already knew. Do you agree?

Boys don't start emotionally disconnected; they often learn it through societal and cultural pressures and what it means to be a man, says Niobe Way, PhD, a researcher, and professor of applied psychology at New York University.

Another expert on the topic, Frank J. Sileo, PhD, founder and executive director of the Center for Psychological Enhancement in Ridgewood, New Jersey, agrees. His 27 years of research on male friendships concluded that men find it hard to express the vulnerability and intimacy needed for close relationships.

Dr. Way goes on to say in her book *Deep Secrets: Boys' Friendships and the Crisis of Connection*, "Men are born with two sides—the hard side is stoic and independent, while the soft side is vulnerable and interdependent. As boys become men, they often become distrustful and embrace their stoic selves, lose friendships, and become emotionally illiterate."

But I have my wife, her friends, and her friends' spouses that I can hang out with for dinner. Isn't that enough? The experts tell us that it may seem like a good solution, but in the long run, it works for neither party. Putting our friendship needs solely on a romantic partner can strain a relationship, not to mention it provides a narrow view of life, with all due respect to my wife.

"It is crucial to have multiple people to go to for support, or even a simple interaction," emphasizes Dr. Chu. Good relationships, from casual interactions, (yes, talking to people on the street) to life partners, make us happier and healthier and lead to longer lives.

But I'm a stoic guy, and I know all about relationships because I read *Men Are from Mars, Women Are from Venus* back in the 90s. But did you really? Or did you skim the headlines, like I did, enough to find out the life-changing discovery that women don't want you to solve their problems; they just want you to listen. A skill that I'm still working on.

We are guys, with that whole "stoic" thing going on, which basically should be a synonym for stubborn, so we need more convincing that this whole relationship is as important as the 84-year Harvard study and loads of studies that confirm the conclusion.

Let's turn to a couple of my favorite topics, history and biology. In the 14th century, so the legend begins, the French scribe Nicholas Flamel and his wife, Perenelle, managed to decode the words of a curious book. Encrypted in the text was a series of instructions that could be used to create an "elixir of life." The words that made them immortal are still true today. The elixir turned out to be that finding someone willing to listen to you may be a real boost to longevity. Yes, you can live longer if you have the right friends, or better yet, be that friend. And the elixir is backed up by biology. In a recent study, fast forward from the ancients to the 21st century, researchers have shown that to build cognitive resilience, surround yourself with people who pay attention to you when you tell stories or need to vent.

The study, published in 2021 in the journal *JAMA Network Open*, found that with strong social support, the best value we can provide in a relationship is to listen. Having someone listen helps our neurogenesis and boosts synaptic plasticity. Essentially, a friend who listens can help make your brain better.

The research concludes that certain neurons involved in brain processes, specifically supported by listening, may make amino acids that contribute to neural repair. The neurons may also be linked to oxytocin production—the love hormone. That makes all the sense in the world. Further support comes from research conducted by *Science in Action* in a study of 2,171 older adults with an average age of 63. (Older by whose standards? I ask.)

The researchers looked at two factors to assess cognitive ability—total cerebral volume and global cognitive scores. The researchers found that people who reported that their friends and family listened to them had a lower risk of cognitive problems. It was also believed that brain health promoted happiness and longevity.

So back to Dr. Waldinger and the ongoing Harvard study. His advice: take stock of your life, the sources of support you have, and what you're getting out of your relationships. Do a relationship assessment of sorts.

Friends, where did you go? I had friends. Are they still my friends? Fair questions. Maybe a good place to start finding answers is by looking at the relationship life of a particular guy ... me. My earliest friends lived on my street, tons of kids of all age groups, and it was easy to find my team. Now I have no idea where they are, except for Jack, my neighbor and first friend, who lives in Texas.

I met Dave, my best friend when we were growing up, at church. We were close. Sixteen years ago, he moved to Florida. I have seen him a few times since he moved, but we talk twice a year on our birthdays. We are still close. But really? Twice a year?

Then came school friends. Each school brought a new set of friends, and I had some carry-over from middle school to high school. Flashback to my reunion, where 150 of my classmates were in attendance. I see two of them on a regular basis. Jeff became my stockbroker, so he had to see me, and Greg and I meet at Miller's, a local burger bar, for our annual catch-up. Annual!

I worked full time during college, I didn't live on campus or attend any activities, so I made no friends. A choice, if given the option, I would have changed. I didn't have the option.

Work friends, like school friends, changed with each job. It was fun while it lasted. I do follow a few careers on LinkedIn; many have posted the wonderful or dreaded word—retired. Depends on your point of view.

Then there were the friends I refer to as "parents of kids' friends." We had great times of shared passion rooting for our kids through all their activities. Football parents are particularly tight. Something about Friday night games has that effect. But then the season ends. I remember telling Mike (one of the parents) on the last game of senior year, "Have a nice life."

I called Mike a few days ago. It was his birthday. I knew that, thanks to Facebook. Our boys have graduated from college.

We've both retired. When I asked, he responded, "I'm having a nice life, thank you so much for calling."

My daughter's sports were different—not as much parental bonding during swim meets (she was a diver), or gymnastics meets, the dads often didn't come. Pole-vaulting was a similar story but for different reasons. The pole vault pit was usually away from the track, far from the other parents, placed behind a shed, or off to the side of the football field. Many pole-vaulters' parents would leave after their kid didn't make their third attempt. We were always there last. As it turns out, all of those years of gymnastics make you a really good pole-vaulter—strong and fearless. My daughter did great, we loved watching, but no friends for us here.

So here I am in a similar situation as many other guys in my age group. I have friends— remember my wife's friends' husbands? And to be fair, I have been able to keep other friendships I have developed along the way. And I value them all. But my assessment does suggest that I, like some of you, need to "up the friend game."

And this is where things are gonna get weird. I'm providing friend advice. But let me assure you, the advice is not from me, a failed friend-maker and friend-keeper. This is advice from the experts. And because I may be veering from our comfortable, stoic feeling arena into the vulnerable soft side of ourselves, I'm going to throw in a whole bunch of useless sports metaphors just to keep us in the game.

Let's start simple, a few laps around the field, court, ice, or whatever metaphoric playing surface you are using to get through this. Who were your friends? Find them and call them. Social media and Google are great places to track down people.

Yes, call them, or use the platform's communication if you don't come up with a phone number.

I called Mark a couple of years ago. We were co-captains on the wrestling team in high school. If there is something that brings people together, it's rolling around on a stinky mat while sweating. We were close until we weren't. He went off to Annapolis to wrestle and be a leader in the US Navy, and I didn't. The call was the first time we had spoken in over 45 years. It was as if life was the same, except it had all changed. But between us, nothing had changed. We were still friends. Can I give a shout-out to the guys that we can do this? I do think it's one of our superpowers. Don't talk for 45 years, and still be friends. We have talked a few times since, and committed to stay in touch.

I think it's time to do a little recruiting and expand the size and talent of our team. And to be sure, this could take us way outside our comfort zone but in many ways have the greatest payoff and expand our world. Find new friends. And for this, we may need a game plan.

First, the basic plays: look at the communities you belong to—church, gym, clubs, activities, and others. Places where common interests can start a conversation. "Do you come here often?" Throw that pickup line away; it didn't work back in the day and is still lame.

I recently made a move at my gym. That sounds weird, but it wasn't. I'm using the move metaphor as in something a running back does to gain yards. I noticed a guy pouring powder into his water bottle, so I asked him what he was drinking. "Amino acids," he said (and you bodybuilders know Amino acids are good for muscle repair). Well, that started a conversation about supplements, health, and even longevity. It turned out that we even have kids the same age. Amp and I now drink green tea once a month at lunch. He is fasting intermittently, and I'm monitoring the process.

Great conversations, each and every one. I'm happier and healthier, and I can just feel the years adding on. Some of our greatest joys are memories of time spent with others. And it's never too late to make new memories.

* * *

When my mom died, we were very worried about my dad. They were so close, and despite his good health, we had always heard stories of a surviving spouse dying from a broken heart. My dad lived for 13 more years after my mom passed.

We were a bit surprised, until last year when I read some of his journals. It was a practice that my dad maintained his entire adult life, or so the box of 72 journals that I found seemed to indicate.

In reading his journals, I found out just how he did it. How he survived for so many years here on earth, knowing that he really wanted to be in heaven with my mom.

Each day his journal entry started the same. I woke up at eight a.m. I spent time in devotion, and I prayed. Then he told the story of his day, what he ate, what he did, and who he talked with. The one consistent element of each day was his spending time with friends. Yes, new friends, people he met since my mom died. Friends that filled the huge void that she left. Friends that he was so grateful for, friends he wrote about every day. I think he would be fine if I shared a few of his entries.

"I went to the café at four p.m. No one ate with me. But Chuck came and sat with me later. I was glad, and we enjoyed our time visiting."

"Bob called. He is coming over for lunch. Bless his heart."

"Bob is such a blessed friend. I truly enjoyed the day. We ate ice cream."

"Doug came by. I'm always happy to see him. He is such a nice person."

"Today had a lot of crooks and turns, but friends made it work. This was such a beautiful day."

My dad was two weeks shy of his 95th birthday when he died. He was a happy man. He had many friends.

* * *

Perfectly good relationships with friends and family can wither and die if they are neglected. As with exercise, we always seem to have an excuse. Life has a way of getting in the way. Let's not let that happen. Yes, our relationships need exercise. We need to work on our relationship fitness. Which relationships energize you? Who do you appreciate? Who do you call that you know will pick up, always? Who listens? Who makes you happy? Call them.

CONVERSATION 21

A Grumpy Old Man

Am I a grumpy old man? I asked my wife shortly after watching *A Man Called Otto* on Netflix. Another amazing Tom Hanks performance. Hollywood loves grumpy old men. Otto is just the most recent of a common theme. The old man loves, experiences loss, turns grumpy, and makes a comeback. Yes, the heart that went into hibernation often for a just cause always seems to make a comeback for a happy ending. But that's Hollywood. At times, I could relate to his character. Rules are meant to be followed, am I right? To be clear, I have never yelled at kids to get off of my lawn, although I have wondered why they don't play on their own. My wife graciously ignored my question, maybe for the better.

Real life offers plenty of reasons for us to get grumpy in our old age. We are not as strong as we used to be; I have aches and pains; my body makes unwanted noises; I stub my toe in the middle of the night on the way to the bathroom; I don't

have the energy I used to have; I don't sleep as well; I can't do
_____ (fill in the blank) as well; I look different; and the
world around me is changing. And I'm just getting started. Did
I touch a few of your "faves"?

Science to the rescue to provide an excuse—scratch that—a
reason for our change in attitude. Men, as they age, experience
a slow and continuous decrease in testosterone production.
This is completely normal, according to Ridwan Shabsigh, MD,
past president of the International Society of Men's Health and
chair, Department of Surgery, St. Barnabas Hospital, Bronx.
But normal doesn't make it good. Low testosterone can have
neural and psychological effects that can lead to low mood
and irritability. Wait, there's more. Low testosterone has many
physical effects on muscle development and, dare I say it, libido
and all that goes on in that category. I could have started and
stopped with this.

There is actually an official medical term for this low testosterone thing. It's called irritable male syndrome. An article
published by the National Institutes of Health provides the
medical definition. Irritable male syndrome (IMS) is a behav-
ioral state of nervousness, irritability, lethargy, and depression
that occurs in adult male mammals following the withdrawal
of testosterone (T). I like the way they abbreviate testosterone
with a T, which I will be using for the remainder of this conversation. They go on with great medical detail to make this
sound very legit, "Changes in the activity of hypothalamic
opioidergic, dopaminergic, and serotonergic neural networks
may dictate the interactive effects of T and photoperiod. The
working hypothesis is that IMS is a transition state associated

with low hypothalamic amine levels triggered, in part, by the withdrawal of opioid peptides."

They could have simply said muscles shrink, sex dwindles, we get grumpy, and most of us would understand. But at least we can say we have a medical condition to explain our poor behavior. Just say you are suffering from IMS, as acronyms are always good when describing a medical condition.

But not everyone agrees. "It's nonsense," says Bradley Anawalt, MD, and chief of medicine at the University of Washington Medical Center. "Older men are irritable—it's almost never due to testosterone." Although science doesn't point to a single answer, some, maybe most (?) do see a link between low T and mood shifts in aging men. I'm wondering how old Dr. Anawalt is. Turns out he is relatively young, so he has lots of time to change his mind.

To solve the dispute, I turned to *The Irritable Male Syndrome: Understanding and Managing the Four Key Causes of Depression and Aggression*, written by Jed Diamond, PhD, and founder of MenAlive, a health program that helps men live longer, healthier lives. It actually did turn out to be a very well-documented source of information. Starting with a logical definition of IMS: "A state of hypersensitivity, anxiety, frustration, and anger that occurs in males and is associated with biochemical changes, hormonal fluctuation, stress and loss of male identity." Good enough, we are back to having a medical diagnosis, not just being jerks. And as with most medical conditions, doctors have recommendations to help cure or minimize the effects of IMS.

Is there a pill? Yes and no. Yes, to solve some of the symptoms (which you already knew), but not to solve the underlying problem. I'm going to stay away from the treatment of low T, that some consider controversial, and focus on the low-hanging fruit, the things that we can do in our daily lives to help with IMS. And the good news is it's the same advice the medical community gives us to live a long, healthy, happy life. Sleep well, eat healthy foods, exercise, stay active, stay connected, reduce stress, and see your doctor. I appreciate the redundancy of this solution. It makes life simple.

Maybe my favorite grumpy old man story is from the movie *Up*. Very much the Hollywood storyline. Carl loved, lost, got grumpy, and made a comeback. Similar to all the other old grumpy men stories, the comeback is brought about by a new relationship with a cat, dog, kid, or neighborhood family. But in each case, the heart that went into hiding comes back to life once we let it.

The story reminds us that as long as we are breathing, life holds the opportunity for countless adventures, which may be occurring right before our eyes.

Here's an idea. Set up a croquet set in the front yard. When the kids walk on the lawn, ask them to join you in a game. Just a thought.

Getting Old Kinda Sucks

This will be the shortest conversation in the book because it's a conversation I didn't want to write. Ironically it was the original title of the book. Why? Well, let me tell you.

When I first started to research "getting old," many of the articles focused on the negative, all the bad things that happen as we age. All the potential physical, mental, emotional, and financial difficulties that could happen. It was mildly depressing. I didn't want to write that book.

Quite by accident, my research results flipped when I ran across the term longevity. Then the focus was all about the potential, the good things that could happen as we age. It opened up an entirely different view, a new vision of the future. And this is a big "and": it revealed that we are not helpless in this journey. This discovery opened my eyes to a better way of living, a better vision of the future, and it led me to change the name of my book. But some stuff does suck; let's get through this.

- Our bodies are different. We look different, feel different, and, for God's sake, our bodies make noises.

- We can't see, hear or taste as well as we used to. I don't love this.

- Pooping can become a problem. Who knew? I didn't until I read one of my grandmother's journals. She would write about three things: doing the laundry and ironing, cooking and food, and if my mother worked that day. She called my mother Babe her entire life. The other thing she recorded was whether or not she went to the bathroom, as indicated by a BM in the upper right corner of each page. On some pages, you would see "BM good one."

- Women have women's issues. And for the guys, we may deal with other personal issues. Both could fill chapters, but let's move on. No family stories to share with you on this topic.

- Our brains have lost some memory and processing speed. I hate it when I can't think of the right word. I tell people I'm trying to think of the French word. I don't know French. And, of course, there is the habit of walking into a room and not remembering what you went in there for.

- Finances can be an issue, the whole fixed income thing. I'm not shy about taking my senior discount wherever it's offered.

- Technology becomes a problem. Thank God we don't have VCR players anymore. I know mine would be blinking.

- I can't find my friends. They are back at work, too busy for lunch, or for some reason, not available. Some permanently.

- When I do get together with friends, we often find ourselves chatting about who is sick, dead, or in the hospital. Yes, we get sick when we get old.

- We start reading obituaries in the paper. There should have been a hard stop when I said the newspaper.

- We live in a country obsessed with youth. Annoying.

- We become invisible. Once people stop needing us, we seem to fade into the woodwork. Hopefully, we can find them when we start needing them.

- There will come a time when things really do suck. We will each face the end of life. I don't have much to say about this, only to suggest that if we live right, this time can be delayed, shortened, and maybe even made easier.

- I'm sure I missed some items and am sorry if I missed yours. But I'm done.

And, yes, getting old does kinda suck. But pause with me for a moment. Was there ever a time in life when some stuff didn't suck? Ah, not so fast. Some stuff sucked big time as a teen, or so it seemed at the time. The pressures of middle age, yeah, sometimes they sucked. So as we approach, or basically are in, this new stage in life, some stuff will suck, just different sucky stuff. Okay, I said it. Are we happy now?

At this time, I could go all Pollyanna on you and suggest reframing the problems and be grateful that we have the opportunity to live another day. But let's get past that because I'm spending too much time on this conversation already.

The bottom line is that we have a couple of options. We can complain and focus on the negative things happening in our lives, making us and everyone around us miserable. Or we can suck it up, count our blessings, and be glad we can wake up tomorrow with the hope of finding a nugget of happiness in our day. We get to choose.

Memories of Metal Cups

I love memories. They make me feel good. On a warm summer day, I will often flash back to my childhood, when our group of friends on the street would play curb ball for hours, and our mothers would stand on the porch and call our names, telling us it was time for dinner. The smallest mother on the street had the loudest voice. You could hear Mrs. Albano for blocks. We would regroup after dinner to continue the curb ball game or add the variety of football or tag until the streetlights came on.

At times I would break away from friends, motivated by the smell of my mom's homemade bread. Nothing fancy, just warm white bread slathered with butter. Along with the bread was a glass of milk that she served in a metal cup that kept the milk cold seemingly forever, even on the hottest days.

I loved those metal cups. I used them at dinner and drank my one allocated Coke per week while watching *The Flintstones* on Friday night. And for something really special, chocolate milk with ice in the metal cup tasted like a Fudgsicle, the kind we could buy from the Good Humor truck that jingled its way down our street most summer afternoons. I shared the stories many times with my kids. I'm sure they enjoyed them, the stories, and the iced chocolate milk I prepared for them on the hot summer days. Well, they liked the chocolate milk anyway.

My love of memories is what drove me to start what's now a family tradition—the memory box. This is much to the chagrin of my wife, who accuses me, and all who follow me, of being pack rats. The infamous memory box is not some small box that sits at the edge of a desk holding a few precious trinkets. Nope, this is the largest plastic container we can find, but it can still fit on a shelf in the basement. Having a rather large basement was a criterion when moving to this house.

I have a couple of boxes that contain memories and treasures from my life. Report cards, trophies, pictures, magazines featuring important life events, favorite records, a Cub Scout book, my first Bible, and many other treasures. It's a special day when I spend a few hours digging through the memories and pausing to laugh at my finds like the high school rules of conduct book. Am I weird?

I have passed the practice on to my kids, only to see them take it to the next level. Although in their defense, they did grow up in the participation trophy generation. That's a lot of trophies.

My son has a few memory boxes mostly filled with sports stuff, including his first baseball mitt, which you have to keep and show to your kids, right? Funny story about his mitt. We thought he was left-handed based on his eating and writing with his left hand. Naturally, we bought him a lefty baseball mitt (which actually goes on the right hand) in order to throw with his left hand. My son wasn't going to be the baseball pitcher we thought; he simply couldn't throw. Until one day: he dropped his mitt and threw a near-perfect strike with his right hand. Yep, ambidextrous, as it turned out. Played all sports right-handed, ate, and wrote horribly with the left hand. Future doctor, we thought. And so it turned out.

Then there's my daughter. Two years younger than my son, she loved her memories and felt the need to fill one memory box for each year of her life. Yep, filled 14 boxes until she outgrew the practice. Lots of memories, which can be a very good thing.

Memories or nostalgic feelings can have some very positive effects on our physical, mental, and emotional well-being. That sentimental feeling of longing for the past can actually reduce pain. Researchers at the Chinese Academy of Sciences and Liaoning Normal University found that observing pictures that triggered childhood memories was linked to participants reporting weaker feelings of physical pain. "People can use nostalgia to reframe their painful experience," says Joe Yazhuon Kong, one of the study's authors. "People can feel happy and peaceful when browsing their pictures."

Other studies have supported the conclusion. A study published in the *Journal of Frontiers in Psychology* showed that nostalgia, triggered by a writing task, decreased the perception of pain intensity among people who suffered from chronic pain.

During this process of nostalgia-induced pain relief, the thalamus plays a critical role. The thalamus, often described as the relay station for the brain, is responsible for passing along sensory information and monitoring signals to the cerebral cortex. The study showed that the thalamus integrates nostalgia information and triggers a pain response that's more controlled.

Other studies have demonstrated the psychological and emotional benefits of memories and feelings of nostalgia. A study in the September 2022 issue of the *Journal of Social Psychology* shows that the more nostalgic one is, the more authentic one feels, which has positive consequences for psychological well-being. Nicholas Kelley, PhD., lecturer in the Centre for Research on Self and Identity, University of Southampton, and one of the leaders of the study, adds, "The results showed a statistically significant increase in all measured components of psychological well-being—social relationships, vitality, competence, meaning in life, optimism, and subjective well-being."

And as it turns out, the more emotional the event, the better the brain is to prioritize memory retrieval. A study published on January 16, 2023, in *Nature Human Behavior* identified a specific neural mechanism in the human brain that tags information with emotional associations for enhanced memory. The team led by Joshua Jacobs, associate professor of biomedical engineering at Columbia University, demonstrated that high-frequency brain waves in the amygdala, a hub for the emotional process, and the hippocampus, a hub for the memory process, are critical to enhancing emotional memories.

Researchers at the California Institute of Technology confirmed the theory and went on to add that one of the ways in which our brain consolidates memories is by mentally reliving the experience. In biological terms, this is the reactivation or replay of neuronal activity patterns associated with a certain experience. The repeated actions make the events more memorable. One of the reasons people hold on to memories so tightly is because they are the one thing that doesn't change when everything else does.

We ask our kids on occasion whether they remember some event from their youth. Often their answer is, "Maybe, but I'm not sure if I remember the event or just the stories I have heard for so many years." I understand.

A 2017 study in *Nature Human Behavior* found that several areas in the brain's prefrontal cortex, areas involved in emotional regulation and cognitive control, became more active when people recalled positive memories. Acute stress lessens our ability to use cognitive and emotional regulation and often triggers anxiety and depression. But thinking about happier times seems to interrupt this cascade of negative thoughts and feelings. Research suggests recalling happier times may be an effective bulwark against stress and depression.

Is anyone else feelin' the positive nature of those memory boxes, or is it just me?

Memories can work in reverse. There is some evidence that suggests people with depression may remember unhappy times as even worse than they actually happened. We keep good and bad memories. We choose mental pathways we want to strengthen and which to allow to grow weaker and eventually dormant.

Then there is "living in the past syndrome," not a medical term, or at least not one that I know of. I remember talking to friends at my high school reunion, which was generally enjoyable. "Catch me up on the last 45 years of your life" was often my lame opening line. And in a matter of minutes, the highlights would be covered: family, career, moves, major life experiences, and even a few references to the Glory Years.

GARRY COLE

But one conversation was different. It never left the memories of high school. Almost like there was nothing worth remembering or talking about in that long 45-year gap. Maybe it was just the nature of the environment or the direction of the chat, but I remember feeling kind of sad as I walked away. I wanted more for this classmate.

Memories have a wonderful way of allowing us to relive the happy moments of our past and to help to create a path to the future. Memories, in many ways, reflect who we are.

I remember going to the theater to watch *The Way We Were* in 1974, one year after graduating from high school. A movie that captured the idea of past memories and a future unfolding. And so it was for me and my classmates at that time in our lives. The title song laid out my path for dealing with memories, although I certainly didn't know it at the time.

> Memories . . .
> May be beautiful and yet
> What's too painful to remember
> We simply choose to forget.

I liked the movie.

Memories are good for me and, as research tells us, good for us all. And the good news: as older adults, we have plenty. Like a good library, we can search the shelves for a favorite to make us feel better or just for pure enjoyment as often as we like. Here is the most important, and maybe most obvious, statement regarding memories. It's never too late to make new memories. It can be a great way to live. Waking up and thinking, maybe I will make a new memory today and then go after it. Who knows, maybe start a new memory box.

* * *

A few years ago, my kids brought metal cups back into my life. For Christmas, they bought me two Moscow Mule cups. Not exactly the metal cups from my youth, but they do the trick of keeping my beverages cold. I drink my beverage of choice, now water, from one of those cups all the time. On more than one occasion during a Zoom work call, I have been accused of "starting the party early, enjoying your Moscow Mule," they would say. I just smile and take a sip. I love my metal cups. Great memories.

Our Purpose in Life

Do you have a purpose in life? This question just seems so big, so ominous. It's the question we may lose sleep over and makes our days anxiety-filled. The question brings equal parts wonder and terror to our minds. We want to put ourselves on the same level as Madam Curie or the Dalai Lama. We want our answer to be . . . big. Well, no. Not all of us will cure cancer, although I'm hoping a team of really smart scientists and doctors will.

Having a purpose in life is very important to our health, happiness, and longevity. But it's less about the magnitude of our purpose and more about our involvement and pursuits. It's what gets us out of bed in the morning.

I asked my wife what her purpose was. She answered very quickly, "To make a difference and wear cute clothes." I love it, and she actively pursues her purpose each and every day. Today, she wore a gray camouflage jacket over a black turtleneck, black stretch pants, and army-like boots. As she was on her way out, I asked her if the difference she plans to make today has to do with a military maneuver. She answered with a snarky laugh. I thought I was hilarious. She did look cute, so for that part of her purpose: check.

No surprise, life is finite and unpredictable. Here, then, is my advice: forget the bucket list. Choose the one thing you like to do, the thing that makes you happy, the thing that you are good at. Keep doing it so you get even better at it and love it even more. Then one day, start to share it with others, and BAM—you have a purpose in life.

My oversimplification, as it turns out, is not that far off from reality. Here's what the experts say. Eminent psychiatrist Viktor Frankl, in his book *Man's Search For Meaning*, wrote, "Woe to him who saw no more sense in life, no aim, no purpose, and therefore no point in carrying on. He was soon lost." A little context may help understand this dramatic need for purpose. Frankl was describing his time in horrible conditions while a prisoner in the Auschwitz concentration camp during WWII. He went on to quote Friedrich Nietzsche, "He who has a why to live can bear any how." It was Nietzsche who also famously said, "That which does not kill me makes me stronger," a phrase we are all familiar with, thanks to Kelly Clarkson and her hit song "Stronger (What Doesn't Kill You)," although the phrase looks far more chilling when written in German: *Was mich nicht umbringt, macht mich stärker.*

Purpose undoubtedly saved Frankl's life. He went on to be a leading psychiatrist introducing the world to a new form of therapy called logotherapy, which is built around the practice of finding meaning and purpose in life. Purpose is important!

In 2014 Robert Butler, MD, founding director of the National Institute on Aging, collaborated with the NIH and found a strong correlation between having a sense of purpose and longevity. A more recent study published by the American Medical Association has linked a strong sense of purpose with a lower risk of all-cause mortality. While the study was based on correlative data, there is evidence that shows that purpose can positively affect our health and longevity.

Richard Leider, author of *The Power of Purpose*, says "One of the greatest secrets of happiness and longevity is living with a sense of purpose. People who wake up with a sense of purpose live (happily) up to seven years longer than those who don't."

How do we find purpose?

According to Leider, the process may not be as complicated as it seems. Developing or uncovering your passion may start with an interest or a curiosity. Start with the question, who are you when you are at your best?

Before we get to the how, let's solidify why we need purpose. Purpose, according to the experts, can deliver on the big three: health, happiness, and longevity. Social research is solid, but what about the science? You know I like my science (so says the guy that squeaked through every science class he has ever taken). Scientific research has shown that purpose at any age may act as a buffer against stress, increasing our well-being and helping to reduce inflammation, which in turn lowers many chronic conditions as we age. Researchers also note several other factors that are found in people with purpose, including positive habits regarding physical and mental health. Having a purpose provides a daily alternative to spending time regretting the past or worrying about the future.

In terms of biological science, stress is a natural response to information we receive about potential danger or problems. The alarm goes off in the brain, sending neurons to the pituitary gland, which in turn produces hormones that release corticotropin that circulates through the sympathetic nervous system. The adrenal gland is triggered to release adrenaline and cortisol. Adrenaline raises our respiratory rate and pulse, while cortisol increases the release of dopamine and blood glucose. This complicated and instantaneous biological reaction was great when a saber-toothed tiger was getting ready to pounce. But ongoing stress, the kind we experience in today's world, has a degenerative effect and causes aging and chronic health conditions over time.

One of the best antidotes for stress is to get out of your own head by focusing on something bigger than yourself. You worry less when you are busy caring about others.

Bring on the purpose. Let's start with a few foundational statements:

- Questions about purpose can never be answered by sweeping statements. Everyone is unique, and our purpose should never be compared to others.

- Purpose will undoubtedly change over time and will often be determined by your given life situation. This takes off a little pressure, I hope. No need for lifelong decisions.

- Definition: What are we even talking about here? Just so we are going in the right direction? Surprise, not even the word *purpose* has a single definition. But let's go with this simple one: the reason why something exists or is done. When we expand this to purpose in life, it varies slightly, depending on whose book you are reading, but the common thought seems to be a central, self-organizing life theme that motivates us to focus on or dedicate time to what is important to us.

What better place to start to learn how to find our purpose than going to college? Vic Strecher, PhD, MPH, is a professor in the Department of Health Behavior Health Education at the University of Michigan (Go Blue!). He teaches a class called Finding Purpose and Meaning in Life. It's also available online and free through Coursera. I took the class and highly recommend it not just because of my affiliation with one of the greatest universities in the world (bias showing intentionally), it's a great class.

Professor Strecher provides a number of thoughts to find your "why" and your purpose. The first step toward unlocking your purpose is to mine your life for threads that reveal your gifts, passion, and values. And never stop being curious. Curiosity is a driving force behind growth.

Ask yourself these questions:

1. What matters to you? What is important?

2. What are your values?

3. Who inspires you?

4. What causes do you care about?

5. What are you grateful for?

6. What are your strengths?

7. What do you like to do?

8. How do you want to be remembered?

He makes two other suggestions in looking for passion and purpose: First, what do you want your headstone to say? Expand that a bit and write your eulogy. It's a bit creepy, but you can get at the essence of who you are and how you want to be remembered. A much simpler task is to look at your phone. What is the picture on your screen? Yep, it worked for me. It's a picture of my kids.

For a real-life application, I would like to return to the Blue Zones, the experts on how to live a long, healthy, happy life. In all the Blue Zones, we find that one of the fundamental reasons for longevity is that the inhabitants live with a sense of purpose. In Okinawa, they embrace a Japanese concept called *ikigai,* which means "that which makes life worth living" or the reason to rise in the morning. This sense of purpose need not be grand or monumental. For many, their reason to rise is to take care of their garden, meet with friends, take care of great-grandchildren, or care for a pet.

Ikigai can often lead to another important Japanese concept called *chanto suru,* which means "properly done." As such, ikigai emphasizes a process and immersion rather than a goal.

Doing something well that is important to you can clearly make life more meaningful. As many of the locals say, it's the joy that guides them through the day.

The people of Okinawa don't stress over finding purpose. They say that their life journey combines three factors from which ikigai will emerge:

- What you love

- What you needed

- What you are good at

Mihaly Csikszentmihalyi might suggest that they have found flow, the state in which they are so involved in the activity that nothing else matters.

Richard Leider, in his book *The Power of Purpose,* has an interesting process to find purpose. He defines it as an equation: Gifts + Passions + Values = Purpose. He defines gifts as your talents, things you are good at. Passions—what you love to do, get excited about and enjoy. Values are the things that are important to you. He goes on to reveal that his purpose in life is to make small, unexpected differences in someone's life each and every day. He looks for "purpose moments," which can be as simple as listening to a friend with full presence.

If you had asked me back in the day if I lived with purpose, my answer would have been no, I just did what I needed to do. In retrospect, I would change my answer because for me, like many others, I just didn't know I had a purpose. And like many others, that changed throughout my life and reflected my situation at that time: getting through school, getting a job, getting married, getting promoted in my job or finding a new one, and so on. Most of us know this pattern. It was very "me" focused.

Not much health, happiness, or longevity here, or so I thought. However, there was a central theme. I always strived to do my best to help myself and those around me. I will say it was that striving, with some success along the way, that brought a sense of well-being and happiness. If I did my best, no need to worry, that's all I could do.

That all changed in 1998 when children came into my life. Many of you may relate to this story. My new purpose in life was to love and take care of my family, plain and simple. Well, not always so simple. No longer "me" focused, it was all about them, which can be dicey at times, especially as kids grow up.

It may be a low aspiration—simply loving and taking care of my family. But in my mind, and the minds of many others, it's truly meaningful. As it turns out, Mother Teresa would agree and would expand our purpose as she once said, "If you want to bring happiness to the world, go home and love your family." Maybe we didn't know it, but we were, and are, helping the world.

One of the wonderful experiences in my life was putting the kids to bed. A bedtime story followed by family prayer. As I walked out of their room, I would put a small yellow submarine (a McDonald's Happy Meal toy) on the edge of their bed. During the night, I would go back to their room and put it back on their desk; this way, they knew that I checked on them during the night. This went on for close to six years, I loved it; I felt like I was fulfilling part of my purpose.

Then one night, it came to a crashing end. After the family prayer, I went to collect my son's yellow submarine from his desk. It was gone. I panicked, but he said calmly, "Dad, I threw it away; you don't need to check on me anymore. I'll be fine." He may have been fine, but I was crushed. Was this the first sign of losing my purpose in life? No, it was the first sign that kids grow up, and my purpose needed to evolve with that fact.

My kids are older now, my son is in medical school, and my daughter is finishing her senior year as an undergrad (they were at the time of this writing). My purpose to love them still remains, but taking care of them continues to evolve, which, at times, is difficult for me. I still check on them every night. GPS trackers on the phone are a wonderful thing. Every night before I go to bed, I check. If they are home, I'm happy that they are safe. If they are out, I'm happy they are having a good time. My daughter accuses me of stalking, but hey, the app found her phone in the middle of the highway a few years back. No, I'm not stalking, I'm still living this part of my purpose, and when I check on them, it makes me happy. This is for me, and I will continue to check on them until "that" day. That day they need to start checking on me.

My job as a father will never be over. I did, and will do, the best I can. Lord knows that I made my fair share of mistakes along the way, but it has been one of the best parts of my journey. There will always be a part of my purpose tied to my family.

Without a doubt, our role in our children's lives now takes less time. It feels like a purpose gap; what am I to do? And oh, by the way, I retired, so that whole job purpose has slipped away too. Yikes! Can anyone relate?

Can we just retire from the purpose thing and take it easy on the last lap? Heck, no. We need to think like an Okinawan. It's never too late to bring purpose to your life. Einstein died while attempting to develop a formula to unite all the forces of the universe into a single theory. He died while living with purpose. Mattering matters from cradle to grave. It's time to repurpose.

I love the repurposing trend in the construction field. In building out the basement in our empty-nest house, I took it to the extreme, maybe subliminally, as I was going through my own repurposing at the same time.

- My bar is made from an old bowling alley.

- A shelf along the wall comprises benches from a high school gymnasium. (My builder said they smelled like butt.)

- The stairway railing was salvaged from the oldest building from Wayne State University, my wife's alma mater.

- The pool table is a 1949 Brunswick Anniversary Edition because I had to have something in the house older than me.

Yes, older things have history and character, and it's exactly those items with special features that deserve to be repurposed. I hope the description of my basement remodel (and its topical metaphor) didn't fall on deaf ears.

This is a great time to find a new purpose in our lives, and maybe for some of us, it's as simple as finding a new need for our old skills and passions.

* * *

I got suckered into being a board member for our neighborhood association. My first project was working on replacing secondary road signs to make them more consistent and attractive. My partner in crime had been a purchasing director at a number of large companies. He's loving this project, talking about supply chain, buying cycles, and purchasing efficiencies. Not my thing, so I'm taking a back seat and letting him drive, and he is enjoying it. He repurposed.

I also find myself harkening back to my past to find my repurpose. No, I'm not bugging my kids, although you may want to get their opinion, and marketing is not top of mind; I didn't even like this year's lineup of Super Bowl commercials.

For me, it has always been about effort, doing my best at something that's important to me. What's important in my life right now? Aging. Yep, if I'm gonna do this, I'm gonna do it to the best of my ability. No regrets, not "I wish I would have done that, knew that, or tried that when I had the chance." Nope, I wake up thinking, how can I make this aging journey the best it can possibly be?

It all started with the research. I needed to know about the big three issues for old people. How can I be happy, healthy, and live a long life? As it turns out, all three rely on each other. And after reading many books and hundreds of articles and listening to hours of podcasts, I have learned many of the best ways to age well.

Now I continue to learn and bore my friends over coffee or lunch. Also, my poor wife, who couldn't care less about aging (the woman who wants to "check out" at 65), has to listen to me daily. So rather than bother them all, I wrote this book with the purpose of sharing thoughts that others may benefit from. I re-purposed; it makes me happy.

Life is better when you wake up with purpose, and that begins with believing you have a purpose. Life is just a series of days strung together. Do you want a good life? Wake up every day and say to yourself, I'm going to do everything in my power to make this a good day. If you wake up tomorrow and you're just not feelin' the purpose, may I suggest you follow my wife's lead? Put on some cute clothes, and go out and try to make a difference.

If Not Now, When?

They say the best time to plant a tree is 20 years ago. And the second best time is now. Let's talk about all those things we wanted to do, wanted to change, or simply things that could make life just a little better. I'm not talking about bucket list stuff, although that could be part of this discussion. No, just the simple things.

Let me share a personal story. As I began to write, the song "All I Ask of You" from *Phantom of the Opera* started to play on my Echo Dot. It's sort of meaningful as my story develops. Feel free to sing along.

In the second verse, the character Christine starts to sing:

> Say you'll love me every waking moment . . .
> That's all I ask of you

Raoul responds:

Then say you'll share with me
One love, one lifetime . . .

Christine:

That's all I ask of you

Yes, down deep inside, I'm a hopeless romantic.

When my wife and I married, we always sat on the couch holding hands for Friday night movies, or she would be draped over me in some fashion. You get the visual. Well, over time, life happens—kids, work, a new house, and a second couch. Yes, a couch for each of us was very comfortable. And life went on for many years.

Then one Friday night, after the kids went off to college and life became less hectic, I peered over at my wife on her couch and realized I missed the hand-holding. The butterflies in my stomach made me think of our first date: Will she like me? Kiss me? Where will this go? I was actually mildly frightened. But I did it. I asked my wife if I could share her couch and we could hold hands. She said no . . . . Just kidding, she said sure. Two years later, and I'm thinking we should sell the other couch.

Your turn. What are those things in your life that you would like to change? Those little things that might make daily life better. Okay, go.

It's hard, I know. Our habits are formed; it's what it is. Life is comfortable. Comfort is often the greatest obstacle to change. Some smart guy once said we have two lives. One starts when we are born. The other starts when we realize that life doesn't last forever. Let's bring this visionary discussion down to a tactical level. Something actionable. Something we can do tomorrow or today. Yep, like *now*. Reading this book can wait.

* * *

Do you remember those God-awful annual reviews at work? The ones that reflected your relationship status with your boss and not really a reflection of your work? Yeah, those. Without bringing back the recurring nightmares, may I suggest a new modified version called "The Little Changes That Will Make My Best Days Ever" plan (still working on the title). Here are my thoughts, but feel free to modify them.

1. Make a list of things in your life that you like, and to each, assign a score of one to ten, with ten meaning you are killin' it, making it happen. And one means it needs a ton of work.

2. Now list all the things that you have always wanted to do, or thought you wanted to do, but don't. Be creative; make this list as big as possible. Don't overlook the little things. (Believe me, eating chocolate on the way home from the grocery can make your day.) Assign a number based on the same system as above.

3. Add up the numbers. This becomes your "best days ever" score.

4. Now, the fun part. The opportunity to increase your "best day ever" score. Pick three things from your lists

that you will add, improve, or eliminate to make life better. Don't overthink this.

Have you read the book *Four Thousand Weeks*? It's a time management book with the reminder that we have 4,000 weeks to live on this earth (give or take, based on the US average life span), so we should make the best of it. Not sure where you stand, but I'm closing in on 3,536 weeks on my next birthday. Yikes.

Armed with a little motivation, I ask: If not now, when?

I will continue to enjoy my Friday nights.

CONVERSATION 26

"Old": It's Time to Rebrand

What comes to your mind when you hear the word "old"? Maybe words like worn, broken, out of date, showing age, or even obsolete. When used in a sentence like "Look at those old people," what do you see? Decrepit, senile, over-the-hill, dull, and boring individuals. Oh good, you didn't see that. Well, I have bad news for you. Some people would.

My friends, we have a brand problem. Our brand image, what people think of as "old" is tattered and torn. It's outdated. It's not accurate. Our brand image doesn't reflect who we are. It's time for a rebrand of the word "old" (when used as an adjective to describe people). Rebrand to move away from undesirable feelings and associations, and allow new perceptions to form. Let's do this!

Let's start with a view of the competition. Unless I'm missing something, the only competition to being old is being dead. I think that makes our competitive position pretty powerful.

181

I would rather be old. Now I know not everyone would agree with that statement, but I think it's safe to assume we are appealing to over 90 percent of our target market.

Sidebar: I'm sorry to speak of death in such a cavalier way and don't mean to offend anyone. I recognize death is very real, very personal, and very sad. But if you will allow me to proceed, you'll see my intentions are honorable.

Back to our brand. Even with such a strong competitive position, we still have lots of work to do. Grab your sticky notes and head to our virtual war room. We have a SWOT analysis to do. Grab your doughnut and prepare to consume the five cups of coffee you'll need for this process. Lunch will be served. This is giving me goosebumps thinking back to my days as a marketer. And we wonder where the extra pounds came from. There were always doughnuts.

SWOT—strengths, weaknesses, opportunities, and threats—a chance for us to throw ideas against the wall to see what sticks. And remember, there are no bad ideas, except there really are, and we always knew it.

Let's jump in. What are the strengths and opportunities of being old, the good things? This will certainly vary based on our circumstances, but for the sake of discussion, I will share my opinion. Because by some definitions, some would consider me to be old. Speaking from experience, I like being old. I'm good at it. Aside from some bumps along the way, I have enjoyed all my ages, so I figure why would this one be any different? And as it turns out, that's a big deal. What we tell ourselves plays a significant role in our health and happiness as we age.

A Boston University School of Medicine and Harvard School of Public Health study published in 2019 suggests that people who tend to be optimistic are more likely to live to be 85 years old or older. The finding is independent of other longevity factors such as socioeconomic status, health conditions, social integration, and other health behaviors.

So what are some of the good things about being old, according to science and me? Discounts, grandchildren, more time, and less anxiety. And yes, according to research, we can be happier. Oh, the list could be greatly expanded, and I will leave that up to you. Use your sticky notes and post on the wall all the good things about being old.

Now what about the bad things about being old—weaknesses and threats? We look different, feel different, people treat us differently, and we have to scroll forever to find our birth year when filling out a form online. And yes, there are more; again, I'll leave it up to you to fill in the blanks. Use a different wall. Maybe a smaller one.

Before we move on, let's talk very briefly about the elephant in the room. One of the most frightening aspects of aging is cognitive decline. I'm not just talking about losing our keys. Heck, I have been doing that since I first got keys. Nope, this is far worse than keys. I could write an entire conversation—others have written books on the topic—and it would be sad to read. But you know me. When backed into a depressing corner, I will redirect the conversation.

According to findings published in the *Natural Human Behavior*, two key brain functions actually tend to improve as we age (catch the redirect, but still on the topic of the brain). Executive inhibition—the ability to focus and reason in order to make effective decisions— actually improve as we get older, with greater awareness of time, place, and self. Yes, we become wiser, and I'm personally looking forward to that kicking in someday.

We have a good start in our rebranding effort. Next, we need a new approach to communication. How can we better talk about and describe "old." I have a thought, a story actually. A few years ago, my wife and I made the decision to move to our empty-nest home. You know, a bit smaller, first-floor primary bedroom, open floor plan, on a smaller lot with a view. A natural step in the aging process. It's not an admission of being old, it's an acceptance of change for the better. You know what I mean. Have you done it yet? It can be difficult for many reasons, but also very freeing.

During the process, we sold some furniture and needed to pick up some pieces to fit in the new home. One of the items needed was a buffet for the dining room, sometimes called a sideboard. Not being a furniture expert, I couldn't determine the difference between the two. I just knew we needed something against the wall and under the lithograph; something with drawers.

My wife suggested I take the lead on the project, so I set out to find something cool. To me, cool would be something old with character, charm, interest, and maybe even a few signs of wear. The options were plentiful, with a wide price range. I understand the concept of getting what you pay for, but I'm just buying a buffet that sits under a painting and holds stuff. They all perform the same basic function, and once I narrowed down the style, they all looked similar.

I found some great pieces on Chairish and 1stDibs, some interesting websites that feature expensive vintage furniture. Very nice stuff, but I kept up the search, although I had my eye on this beautiful, expensive piece. It only hurts once when you pay, or so I told myself.

And then I discovered something interesting in the back corner of a local resale shop, beyond the good stuff. There was a buffet, the same size, shape, and similar design as the expensive ones, but this was priced at only $95. Yes, it needed work, a lot of work, but I was still surprised at the deal. I asked the shop owner why it was so cheap. (Maybe not a smart move in advance of the upcoming barter.) "It is old," she said. And there it was; the difference between $95 and $2,900 is best described in the choice of the word, *old* versus *vintage*.

We need to explore this a bit. Two pieces of furniture filling the same basic need and chronologically around the same age with much different value. Yes, the physical condition was part of the answer, but the choice of the word used to describe the furniture absolutely affected the brand image.

I bought the old buffet for $95, the asking price. I didn't even try to barter, the piece deserved the respect of full price, not that I could have done better, given my approach.

I had it refinished. The buffet came back stained in elegant flat black, the best choice to hide the years of wear. Gold high-lighted the trim. Perfect for the room and pulling out colors from the Peter Max litho that was displayed above on the wall.

The handles and drawer pulls were original, a bit bent, and one was missing. My refinisher asked if I would like new handles. I said no; the originals reflected the age, charm, and personality of the piece. It wasn't perfect, and it shouldn't be. It reflects the characteristics that make it unique and special. It's vintage.

185

Yes, one giant furniture metaphor to describe the T-shirt that we should all start wearing: "I'm not old. I'm vintage."

I love the word vintage. It's such a powerful word and fun to say. And when used to describe cars, clothes, cards, and wine, it has the same effect as furniture. It makes everything so much more expensive and more valuable. And I have another story about a T-shirt.

On a recent trip to San Francisco, I went to Haight-Ashbury. I had to do it. It was one of the main centers of counterculture in the 1960s. The community was the gathering spot for hippies that created a social experiment that would spread throughout the nation. The ideals were drugs, music, and love—free love— as I remember wondering about it as a young teen.

The first head shop opened on January 3, 1966, offering a spot to purchase drug paraphernalia and other things, maybe from the back room. Others followed.

The music culture exploded with area bands like the Grateful Dead, Big Brother and the Holding Company, and Jefferson Airplane all immortalizing the neighborhood in song.

I had to see this place for myself. I grew up hearing about its iconic lifestyle, and, in a small way, it shaped my life. We all had a little hippie in us at the time.

I was not disappointed. Let me be clear, this is not the Haight-Ashbury of the '60s, but ghosts of the past were all around, along with souvenir shops selling every possible tchotchke related to the times. I bought a Christmas ornament of a colorful bus resembling that of the Grateful Dead. It's cool to me.

But I needed souvenirs for the kids, not that they would appreciate the Haight-Ashbury experience as we would. Heck, they may not even know what a hippie is. But they can always wear a T-shirt.

I could have bought one from the tchotchke shop for $14.99, but no, I wanted something more authentic. So I stopped by one of the many vintage shops that proliferate Haight Street. They are so cool. ReLove Vintage, a great name, I thought, is right near the corner of Haight and Ashbury, across the street from Ben and Jerry's (perfect).

And they had T-shirts—vintage T-shirts reflecting the period they were known for and I lived through, the fabulous 60s. I found the shirt- Grateful Dead Band, the perfect hippie shirt. One thing about vintage clothing shops, at least in my limited experience, is they don't tend to mark the items with prices. I, therefore, asked the young hippie (yes, they have young hippies now) how much the shirt was. "Two hundred and forty-nine dollars," she responded, and went on to explain the style, make, and design and reflected on the effect that Jerry Garcia had on the era. All very interesting, but $249 for a T-shirt?

I mentioned that I'm fond of the word vintage as a way to describe us. We are not just old. We have style. We are in decent shape. We reflect a special time in history, and yes, we have value. I bought my kids the $14.99 shirt from the tchotchke shop, but, boy, did I covet that Grateful Dead shirt.

Vintage: of old, recognized, and enduring interest, importance, or quality. Of high quality and lasting values, showing the best and most typical characteristics of a particular time. Classic, warm, real, true, authentic. These are the words that describe us. Yes, we are not old, we are vintage. Wear the T-shirt.

* * *

As with any good brand project, we need to hear from our target audience. As is the case with most brands, the attitude toward old is all over the board. But in looking at the data, we find an interesting pattern. It appears that we in Western societies, more specifically in the United States, have a somewhat unique take on getting old. We think it sucks, and the reminders can be found all around us. Apparently, we have an excuse for such a negative take on the aging process. It gets back to our ancestors and the good ol' Protestant work ethic. I have nothing against the Protestants, and yes, they believed hard work would make you successful. But it was that success attributed to work that provided value in one's life, and once it was gone, your value followed.

Other countries and cultures feel differently. Pulitzer Prize-winning author Jared Diamond, in his book *The World Until Yesterday*, describes vast differences in how societies view and treat senior citizens. Some groups revere and respect their oldest members, while others see them as senile, incompetent, and a burden on society. Ouch.

The perceived value of the elderly is an important factor in determining if seniors are respected or not. In China, it's illegal to neglect your elderly parents. The Law passed in 2013 named Protection of the Rights and Interest of Elderly People states that adult children should never neglect their parents and should visit them often or suffer fines or jail time.

In France, parents are also protected by law. A decree passed in 2004 (Article 207 of the Civil Rights Code) requires citizens to keep in touch with their geriatric parents. A law that admittedly is often difficult to enforce.

When I was discussing this with my friend Amp, he became flabbergasted, a word my dad used, but you may not have heard in a while, but it works well in describing his reaction. He said, "I can't believe there needs to be laws for people to care for their parents." Great reaction.

Amp's parents are from India, and even though he was born in America, he still reflects the values of his ancestry. In India, the elder continues as the head of the household, often lives in a multigenerational home, and takes care of the grandchildren while the younger adults go to work. The opinions and wisdom of the elders are often the final word in family affairs. And family is a high priority.

In Scotland, older people are considered an asset and actively participate as family leaders. In 2011 the government introduced a program called Reshaping Care for Older People that aimed to improve care and meet the challenges of an aging population.

Japan leads the world in embracing its seniors. This is clearly reflected in the fact that they have the longest life span and report living happier as they age.

I think we are closer than we think to flipping this paradigm. Old is not always a bad thing, and to some people, it never was.

* * *

I have a thought that I would like to share. One of the many positive attributes of aging, besides optimism for some, is wisdom. And one element of being wise is not giving a shit about what others think. What matters at this time in our lives is what *we* think. Let me ask you: Does old suck, or are you going to take full advantage of this freedom to be old?

Brand image, my friends, reflects what the audience thinks of the brand, in some cases, regardless of the reality. How we feel about being old should only matter to one person—you. And we need to get out of our self-imposed shells to discover what others in our world think about being old—it's celebrated.

Stop skipping birthdays, 50 is not the new 60, and start living your days the best way possible for you. It's never too late to start having a good day. And we will never have another now.

I think back to the football game when the high school kids yelled, "Hey, look at the old people." Do you remember my story of the reunion? Yeah, that game. I wish I had the wisdom then to think, Yep, that's me. Old is better than dead. Better yet, I wish I had the T-shirt.

Longevity According to Artificial Intelligence

This may have been my favorite conversation to write because…I didn't write it. Yes, friends, I have officially entered the 21st century. I used ChatGPT, an artificial intelligence platform, to write it. This is the only writing from AI in this book. But I wanted to try it and share the results with you.

I have been intrigued with artificial intelligence since watching *Westworld* (1973). Did you see it? *Westworld* flashed forward to 1983, featuring a high-tech adult amusement park populated by lifelike androids with whom to interact. Nothing says "the shit is gonna get real" like lifelike androids. And it did. Apparently, AI was something to fear back in the 70s.

As it turns out, *Westworld* was one of many films with elements of artificial intelligence, though certainly not the first. Let the record show that *Metropolis* (1927) was the first movie to involve AI. No, I didn't see it at the time of its release, but thanks for asking. Don't we all like to make aging jokes on occasion?

This German expressionist science-fiction silent film was set in a dystopian future. It follows Freder, the son of the wealthy city master, as he attempts to overcome the vast gulf separating the classes in society. Critics panned the film at the time for being naive, silly, and promoting a communist message. But most people thought the film was too long (153 minutes). Wow, to all of that.

Back to me and my first attempt at using artificial intelligence for writing. It was fun, fast, and interesting. I'd like to point out it returned very little new information regarding the topic of human longevity beyond what my research had already uncovered. It just did it way faster. I'll warn you that most of what you are about to read has already been covered in other areas of the book. This just presents it in a much more matter-of-fact way. Maybe better written, but not as fun to read, in my humble opinion.

Also, it will read a bit choppy. The platform I used only returned four to six paragraphs per request. So I kept asking questions to delve deeper. I didn't add any transitions because I wanted to provide an unadulterated view of what artificial intelligence has to say about the topic of human longevity. So here you go:

> Human longevity refers to the length of time a human being can live. While the maximum human life span is believed to be around 120 years, the average human life span varies depending on factors such as genetics, lifestyle, and environmental factors.

The study of human longevity is a multidisciplinary field that involves genetics, biology, medicine, and social sciences. Researchers are interested in understanding the biological and genetic factors that influence aging and longevity, as well as the environmental and lifestyle factors that affect health and life span.

While there is no single "magic pill" for extending human life span, research has identified a number of factors that can help promote healthy aging and increase the chances of living a longer, healthier life. These factors include maintaining a healthy diet, engaging in regular exercise, avoiding smoking and excessive alcohol consumption, managing stress, and staying socially connected. Additionally, advances in medical research and technology are leading to new treatments and interventions that may help extend human life span in the future.

There have been numerous scientific and technological advances in recent years that have the potential to lengthen human life span. Some of these include:

1. Genetic engineering: Advances in genetic engineering have made it possible to identify and modify specific genes that are associated with aging and age-related diseases. This technology holds the potential to extend life span and improve overall health.

2. Stem cell research: Stem cell research has shown promise in regenerating damaged tissues and organs, which could potentially extend life span by reducing the effects of aging and age-related diseases.

3. Artificial intelligence: Artificial intelligence has the potential to revolutionize health care by enabling personalized medicine and more precise diagnoses, which could lead to better treatment outcomes and ultimately extend life span.

4. Antiaging drugs: Researchers are currently investigating a range of drugs and compounds that have shown promise in extending life span and improving overall health in animal studies. These drugs could potentially be used in humans in the future.

5. Nanotechnology: Nanotechnology holds the potential to develop targeted therapies for age-related diseases, which could improve treatment outcomes and potentially extend life span.

It's important to note that while these advances hold great promise, there are still many challenges to overcome before they can be widely implemented. Additionally, ethical considerations must be taken into account when developing and implementing these technologies.

There is currently no single "best" antiaging drug or treatment that can significantly extend human life span. However, there are several drugs and compounds that have shown promise in animal studies and are being studied for their potential to extend human life span. Here are a few examples:

1. Metformin: This is a drug that's commonly used to treat type 2 diabetes. Studies in animals have shown that metformin can extend life span and improve overall health, and there is ongoing research to determine whether it has similar effects in humans.

2. Rapamycin: Rapamycin is an immunosuppressant drug that has been shown to extend life span in animals. It works by inhibiting a protein called mTOR, which is involved in cell growth and metabolism. However, more research is needed to determine whether it has similar effects in humans.

3. NAD+ precursors: NAD+ is a molecule that plays a key role in energy metabolism and has been shown to decline with age. Researchers are investigating compounds that can increase NAD+ levels in the body, which could potentially slow down aging and extend life span.

4. Resveratrol: Resveratrol is a compound found in red wine and grapes that has been shown to extend life span in animals. However, more research is needed to determine whether it has similar effects in humans.

It's important to note that the effectiveness and safety of these drugs and compounds are still being studied, and it's not yet clear whether they can significantly extend human life span. Additionally, it's important to consult with a health care professional before taking any new medications or supplements.

There is currently significant research being conducted into the development of antiaging drugs and compounds. Some of the most promising areas of study include:

1. Senolytics: These are drugs that target senescent cells, which are cells that have stopped dividing but continue to release harmful molecules. Senolytics are being studied for their potential to delay or reverse age-related diseases.

2. Metformin: This is a drug that's currently used to treat type 2 diabetes, but it has also been shown to have potential antiaging effects. Researchers are studying the use of metformin in healthy individuals to determine if it can increase life span and improve overall health.

3. Rapamycin: This is a drug that's used to prevent organ rejection in transplant patients, but it has also been shown to have antiaging effects in animal studies. Researchers are studying its potential use in humans for antiaging purposes.

4. NAD+ boosters: NAD+ is a molecule that plays a key role in energy metabolism and cellular repair. Researchers are studying compounds that can increase NAD+ levels in the body to see if they can improve health span and life span.

5. Caloric restriction mimetics: These are compounds that mimic the effects of caloric restriction, which has been shown to extend life span in animal studies. Researchers are studying the potential of these compounds to delay or reverse age-related diseases in humans.

Overall, there is significant interest and investment in the development of antiaging drugs and compounds, and it's likely that we will see more breakthroughs in this field in the coming years.

There are many factors that contribute to a long and healthy life, some of which are within our control and others that are not. Here are some of the most important things people can do to increase their chances of living a long and healthy life:

1. Eat a healthy diet: A diet that is rich in fruits, vegetables, whole grains, lean proteins, and healthy fats can help to reduce the risk of chronic diseases such as heart disease, diabetes, and cancer.

2. Exercise regularly: Regular physical activity can help to maintain a healthy weight, reduce the risk of

chronic diseases, improve bone density, and improve mental health.

3. Get enough sleep: Getting enough sleep is important for overall health and can help to reduce the risk of chronic diseases such as heart disease and diabetes.

4. Manage stress: Chronic stress can have negative effects on health, so it's important to find healthy ways to manage stress, such as through exercise, meditation, or spending time with friends and family.

5. Don't smoke: Smoking is a major risk factor for many chronic diseases, including lung cancer, heart disease, and stroke. Quitting smoking is one of the best things you can do for your health.

6. Limit alcohol consumption: Drinking too much alcohol can increase the risk of liver disease, cancer, and other health problems. It's recommended that men consume no more than two drinks per day and women consume no more than one drink per day.

7. Stay socially active: Maintaining social connections can help to reduce stress and improve mental health, which can have positive effects on overall health.

While there is no surefire way to guarantee a long life, adopting these healthy lifestyle habits can go a long way toward improving your chances of living a long and healthy life

The maximum human life span is currently unknown, and it's difficult to make accurate predictions about how long humans can live. However, scientific studies suggest that the human life span may be able to reach up to 120 years or even slightly beyond.

Currently, the oldest recorded human life span is 122 years and 164 days, achieved by Jeanne Calment of France, who lived from 1875 to 1997. Some researchers believe that as medical advancements continue, and we learn more about aging and how to slow down the aging process, humans may be able to live even longer.

However, it's important to note that even if humans can live longer, it doesn't necessarily mean that all people will be able to achieve these maximum life spans. Many factors, such as genetics, lifestyle choices, and environmental factors, can affect how long a person lives. Additionally, quality of life is just as important as quantity of life, and many people prioritize having a high quality of life in their later years over living to an extremely old age.

There is no single factor that can predict human longevity with absolute certainty, as life expectancy is influenced by a complex interplay of genetic, environmental, lifestyle, and social factors. However, one of the strongest predictors of human longevity is healthy lifestyle habits, including regular exercise, a balanced diet, adequate sleep, stress management, and avoidance of harmful behaviors such as smoking and excessive alcohol consumption.

Studies have consistently shown that people who adopt healthy lifestyle habits are more likely to live longer than those who do not. For example, one study found that people who engaged in moderate physical activity, didn't smoke, maintained a healthy weight, and ate a healthy diet had a 63 percent lower risk of death than those who didn't engage in these behaviors.

Other factors that can contribute to longevity include access to high-quality health care, education, social support, and a sense of purpose and fulfillment in life. Overall, a combination of healthy lifestyle habits and social and environmental factors is likely to have the greatest impact on human longevity.

Genetics can play a significant role in human longevity, as certain genetic variations have been associated with an increased or decreased risk of age-related diseases and mortality. Some people are genetically predisposed to live longer than others due to factors such as more efficient DNA repair mechanisms, enhanced immune function, and better stress response systems.

Studies of centenarians (people who live to be 100 years or older) have identified several genetic variations that are more common in this population, including variations in genes involved in inflammation, cell growth, and DNA repair. However, it's important to note that genetics is only one factor that influences longevity, and it's not the only determinant of how long a person will live.

Environmental and lifestyle factors such as diet, physical activity, stress, and exposure to toxins can also play a significant role in determining how long a person lives. In fact, studies suggest that lifestyle factors are likely to have a greater impact on longevity than genetics. Therefore, even if a person has a genetic predisposition to live longer, adopting healthy lifestyle habits is still important for maximizing their life span and maintaining good health in their later years.

The percentage of human longevity that's attributed to genetics is still a topic of ongoing research and debate among scientists. It's difficult to estimate the exact percentage, as longevity is influenced by a complex interplay of genetic, environmental, and lifestyle factors.

Studies of families with a high prevalence of centenarians (people who live to be 100 years or older) suggest that genetics may account for approximately 20 percent to 30 percent of the variability in human life span. However, this is just an estimate, and it's important to note that genetics alone cannot determine how long a person will live. Environmental and lifestyle factors such as diet, physical activity, stress, and exposure to toxins can also play a significant role in determining life span and health outcomes.

Therefore, even if a person has a genetic predisposition to live longer, it's still important to adopt healthy lifestyle habits and engage in preventive health behaviors in order to maximize life span and quality of life.

The desire for a long and healthy life varies widely among individuals and is influenced by a variety of personal, cultural, and social factors. However, studies suggest that many people express a desire to live a long and healthy life and that their desired life span may be influenced by their perception of aging, health status, and quality of life.

In general, studies suggest that people in developed countries tend to desire a longer life span than people in developing countries. According to a survey conducted by Pew Research Center, the majority of adults in the United States, Europe, and Japan expressed a desire to live to be 90 years or older. However, the desire for a longer life span may be tempered by concerns about the quality of life in old age, such as poor health, social isolation, and financial insecurity.

Ultimately, the desire for a long and healthy life is highly personal and may be influenced by a variety of factors such as personal goals and aspirations, cultural and societal expectations, health status, and family history.

* * *

Okay friends, there you have it. Longevity, according to artificial intelligence. So, what do you think? Did AI get it right?

A little dry and redundant, but accurate information. I highly encourage you to give AI a try on any topic you want to learn about. The tool that I used was quick and easy: https://chat. openai.com/chat. The examples I used for search topic options were as follows: (1), Explain quantum computing in simple terms; (2) Got any creative ideas for a 10-year-old's birthday?

Well, that pretty much runs the gamut. Good luck, and have fun with your new friend. I will see you in the next conversation where I will be writing again. Yep, back to me.

10 Pillars to Living a Happy, Healthy, and Long Life

This is a big topic. Another five-cups-of-coffee topic. This is as close as we are going to get to the mythical fountain of youth. As it turns out, it's not a place; it's a process. I hope no one is disappointed or surprised. It's a very difficult process that demands a great deal of effort on our part. But well worth our time. Are you with me?

Yes, genetics is important, but not as much as we once thought, only 20 percent to 40 percent depending on which study you read and how long you wish to live. To become a centenarian, you need a little extra help from your DNA. But here's the good news, no, really great news. How we choose to live our lives plays a significant role in whether we are going to be happy, healthy, and live a long time. We are very much in control, and who doesn't applaud that?

It's important to note that I have combined three life goals in this quest. The reason may be obvious to most, but it's worth mentioning. Not everyone wants just a long life (ask my wife), although research would suggest otherwise. But when you add happiness and health to the mix, we would all say, yes, let the party begin.

May I continue to be Mr. Obvious and point out that these goals and the pillars that follow don't apply solely to us older adults? No, this is a solid life plan for people of any age. We are never too young or too old to make good life choices that can make us happier and healthier with the byproduct of living a long life.

Roger Landry, MD, agrees with me. In his book *Live Long, Die Short,* he says, "How we age is up to us. The choices we make every day determine if our lives will have a long degrading decline or a time of continued growth and the highest possible functioning for as long as possible."

Dr. Landry goes on to cite the groundbreaking MacArthur study published in 1987 by John Rowe and Robert Kahn, which found that successful aging (throughout life) decreased the risk of chronic disease, higher levels of overall function, and a shorter period of decline. This result was primarily due to lifestyle choices in which high physical and mental activity are the norm, as are lowering health risks and staying engaged with life.

I was very purposeful in my choice of the term *pillars* in describing what we need to do to achieve this lofty life of health, happiness, and longevity. My wife didn't like the term, it sounds too corporate-y she said. Well, then, give me a better word, I asked. Her sarcastic response was *buttresses.* I think I will stay with pillars.

Dr. Landry uses the word *tips* to describe how to achieve successful aging. Fine for him, but "tips" just doesn't feel strong enough. What I'm about to share is too important to be called "tips." Tips are what you get at the horse track on which horse is going to win the next race. Pillars deliver the feeling of strength that I'm looking for.

Pillars also provide the metaphoric imagery that's important to this story. Pillars need to work together and support each other. If one pillar starts to crumble, it puts pressure on the others. The other pillars will hold for a while but will start to be affected over time.

As you will soon see, each of the pillars supports all three of our goals—health, happiness, and longevity. As a matter of fact, the three goals support each other. Oh, the beauty of this conversation. Yes, health and happiness work together and, in tandem, lead us to a long life.

Many longevity experts use the term health span in describing the interplay. It sounds much better than longevity, even to my wife, who has been clear about the prospects of failing health in old age. "Live long, die short," is a wonderful mantra from our friend Dr. Landry. Isn't that what we all would like?

So how do we achieve this panacea for being happy, healthy, and having a long health span? We're almost there. But I need to add the following disclaimer and clarification.

The 10 pillars are not my own. They are the distillation of loads of research from experts in the field. As I tell my kids, "Don't take my word for it, just listen to the experts." Oh, and this was fun. I used AI to fact-check my work. Yes, after I wrote this conversation, I asked chat.openai.com how people can live happy, healthy, and long lives. I asked the question four times in slightly different ways to ensure accuracy and completeness. And BAM, my research and the following list proved to be solid. Without further ado, here goes:

The Ten Pillars to Living a Happy, Healthy, and Long Life (Health Span)

1. Live as Healthy as Possible

I qualify "as healthy as possible" to recognize that genetics and luck are factors in our health. But the good news is that we can play a significant role in this pillar with our lifestyle choices.

When my kids were growing up, I would tell them "If you want to grow up to be big and strong, you need to sleep well, eat well, and exercise. Well, it appears my advice is scientifically accurate for people of any age.

I have not discussed health much in our earlier conversations, nor am I going into detail now. My goal was to write one book, not the many it would take to cover the topic in detail. Besides, they are written, and I encourage you to read as many as you can. But let me highlight a few key points in bullet point fashion (easier to skim or skip).

- Sleep: Get seven to nine hours of healthy sleep per night. Please read about healthy sleep, it's the bedrock of a healthy lifestyle. It's essential for cognitive function, mood, physical health, and healthy relationships.

- Nutrition: Do you remember the good ol' days when we ate according to the food pyramid, and breakfast was the most important meal of the day? Oh, how I miss my bacon and eggs, reading the back of the Cheerios box, or grabbing frosted strawberry Pop-Tarts on the run. Now I'm intermittently fasting and loving my Mediterranean diet. Nutrition is very personal. My friend Tim has had huge success with a keto diet. I admit I'm jealous watching him eat his meat and eggs as I dip my spoon into my flavorless plain Greek yogurt. We both feel good after we eat, so whatever works.

- Exercise: I finally went back to the gym after my two-year COVID-19 break. This is hard, but we have options. Do you remember the people in the Blue Zones? They don't go to Planet Fitness. Their life is full of movement. Walk to a friend's, bike to town for groceries, chase great-grandchildren, and spend hours in the garden. The key here is to wear your Nikes and "Just Do It."

- Avoid unhealthy behavior: I'll try not to sound too "preachy" here, but as a quick reminder, I was raised Southern Baptist. Maybe our pastor should have told us smoking and drinking too much was bad for our health. A little red wine is fine. You do remember Jesus's first miracle, right? Hallelujah.

- Consider supplements: another quick reminder, I'm not a doctor or health care professional. This, nor any statement I make, is not meant to be medical advice. You should always consult your doctor before trying any supplement or making any changes to your lifestyle. With that disclaimer out of the way, consider supplements to complement a healthy diet. Apparently, we don't absorb nutrients as well when we age, so packing more in with multivitamins or the nasty-tasting green drink may help.

- And what about the magic pills, the antiaging fountain-of-youth pills? Read about them in conversation 30. Be prepared for an even longer disclaimer.

That's our first pillar. I wanted to start with an easy and obvious one to get us going. Longevity experts suggest a healthy lifestyle may deliver some of the most powerful effects on our goals.

2. Get Your Relationship Game Going

Yes, this makes it to the top ten list. Remember that Harvard study? Check out conversation 20. The bottom line here: relationships make us happy and healthy and help us live longer. Apparently, love does make the world go 'round; many extra revolutions if you do it right.

3. Live with Purpose

I considered claiming this to be the most important pillar because of all the intrinsic value it brings to someone's life. I didn't because of people's reactions to the topic. Not just in my little circle, but the grander statistic suggesting that up to 75 percent of people in the United States don't feel they have a purpose.

May I suggest that they do but just don't think or talk about purpose in life? We talk about work, family, spirituality, vacation, and hobbies. Each or any combination could very well be one's life purpose. I have been boring people with my talk about research and writing for almost two years now. I have been asking myself, what happens when I'm done writing? Yikes!

Purpose can be frightening or exhilarating. Check out conversation 24 to see if your reason for waking up in the morning could use a tune-up or rediscovery.

4. Manage Anxiety

Just calm down! Have you ever used that phrase in the heat of an argument? Did it work well? I didn't think so. But there are some positive things we can do to manage our own anxiety. But please, unless you are a trained professional, don't try to manage someone else's.

This is the pillar we find ourselves patching, fixing, or holding up just to get through the day. Anxiety finds a way to creep into all of our lives in so many ways. Everything is going well until you get the phone call, then another. The brain kicks in, and the biological process starts. And if anxiety becomes chronic, the inflammation it causes starts to affect other pillars. As we know, it happens. Life happens.

Read, research, or find help. We all need to find a way to manage anxiety. In the meantime, let's go for a walk. The experts say it does wonders.

5. Stay Curious

In one of the most compelling commencement speeches of all time (40 million views on YouTube), Steve Jobs in 2005 concluded his address by telling Stanford graduates to "stay hungry and stay foolish." I don't think Jobs was suggesting intermittent fasting at the time or becoming a comedian. He was challenging this elite group to look forward, to challenge themselves, and, yes, to be curious, as he was in his own life. His words didn't apply only to the 20-somethings starting their journey. He may not have been thinking specifically about it at the time, but staying curious is great advice to people of any age.

Super-agers are people in their 80s and beyond who have the cognitive function of those decades younger. According to a 2021 study from Harvard Medical School, led by Professor of Neurology Alexandra Touroutoglou, who followed a group of super-agers for 18 months, found they kept learning new things throughout their lives. Like a bank account, they keep making deposits of new information, which helps make new connections between brain cells.

Yes, to be curious, to exercise your brain, to continuously learn and expand your world, and maybe most important, to wonder about tomorrow and what it will bring.

6. Be Optimistic

This one may come as a surprise to some. As such, it deserves its own conversation. Check it out in conversation 29.

7. Keep Your Head in the Game

Brain Health: it may be the elephant in the room. The topic that no one wants to talk about and I did not want to write about. I even tried to lighten the mood by naming this pillar after a song from the popular teen movie *High School Musical*.

But as has been the case throughout this book, I bring some positive news to the topic. The other pillars will help hold this one up. Yes, the best way to keep our minds strong is the same way we keep our bodies strong. Sleep well, eat well, and exercise. Oh, and work hard on all of your other pillars as well. They will all work together to keep this one propped up.

But most important, exercise your brain. Dedicate that dining room table that you do not use anymore to the biggest puzzle you can find. As you painstakingly assemble it, you will enjoy the beauty of your work and the expanding visual. For me, it may be the Amalfi Coast or a giant picture of my family. Or crossword puzzles or sudoku. But for many of us, it's reading.

As it turns out, what we read may make a difference. Many years ago, my daughter brought home a cute Father's Day card she made in school. Offering a description of me, she wrote, "My dad likes to read . . . the mail." Well, she might be happy to know that I worked my way up to articles and now to books. Yes, I read now, which is a good start.

My wife, on the other hand, is a prolific reader. I asked her, as one with so much experience, to read my book. She liked it, except for the references to herself, she humbly said. Then I asked her if she would buy it. Much to my dissatisfaction, she responded without hesitation, "No. I don't read self-help books," she said.

She reads fiction of all forms. Well, as it turns out, reading fiction may just be one of the best "self-help books" for our brains. Richard Restak, MD, an 81-year-old neuroscientist and clinical professor of neurology at George Washington University School of Medicine and Health Sciences tells us, "Fiction requires you to exercise your memory as you proceed through the plot. It is critical to retain a variety of details, characters, and subplots." My wife has been reading self-help books all along. Maybe she'll buy mine; maybe I'll sign it.

8. Know Your Doctors' Names

It used to be easier when I had only one name to remember. But even his name was a bit difficult— Dr. Samuel Jonnalagadda. I made it easy, Dr. Sam. Everyone calls him Dr. Sam.

My team of doctors has expanded. Now I also have a dermatologist, cardiologist, and once a year check in with Dr. Sam. I don't see them often enough to remember their names, or so is my excuse. But that's not the point. The point is to see doctors on a regular basis to prevent the bad stuff from happening.

I once blew up my wife's car. No, not on purpose. I let the engine oil run dry. How stupid of me. But the car was running okay, and who knew the Check Engine light wasn't working? I'm not a car guy, but I should have taken preventive measures. Listen to that little noise; check out that small pain. Go in for that scheduled checkup and maintenance so that someday things just don't blow up.

I still don't know anything about cars; not my thing, so best to leave it to the experts. And as you may have picked up, I'm no longer talking about cars.

9. Go to Church

Any church, any religion. Science doesn't care. Go into the woods and meditate with your own God. My religious friends will take issue with this suggestion, but I'm not here to argue about religion. The research (see conversation 15) strongly supports the idea that spirituality leads to a happier, healthier, and longer life. And for that, we award it a pillar.

10. Enjoy Life

"I finally figured out the only reason to be alive is to enjoy it," said American feminist writer Rita Mae Brown. This is a rather obvious yet introspective quote from the 78-year-old. (She is one of us.) But have we really figured it out? I mean how to enjoy life. Are we enjoying life as much as we could be?

What we do to enjoy life is a personal matter. As I think about the activities of my friends, sometimes I think that sounds fun and at other times, the phrase "no freakin' way" comes to mind. Clearly, the right approach to the topic would be to each their own.

* * *

There is a process to enjoying life that will be relevant to us all. A way to enjoy life to its fullest and, yes, make us happier, healthier, and have a longer health span, thus cementing the concept of enjoying life as our tenth and final pillar.

Eleanor Roosevelt said, "The purpose of life is to live it, to taste the experience to the utmost." She simplifies such a magnanimous life goal into a simple expression of "taste the experience." As one who enjoys eating, a family trait I inherited from my father and have since passed down to my son, the use of the word taste is relatable to me. But it's the word "utmost"— the striving for the best, the extreme, the greatest possible—that's my focus and how we can enjoy life to the fullest.

In the United States, the home of fast food and the lunch hour, we don't know how to eat. We eat to live and, in many cases, overeat because of portion size—a topic for a different conversation.

GARRY COLE

On our first family trip to Europe, we learned how to eat. In Italy, lunch lasted for hours, and dinner went past my wife's bedtime. I loved it. And Barcelona was even better. After that long lunch came siesta time. Annoying for us American travelers who found many of the shops closed in the afternoon, but I appreciated the culture and the lifestyle.

The word that crept into my mind as I walked through the crowded streets and saw people really enjoying themselves and each other was "savor." Being in the moment and enjoying every element of the moment. By definition, savor means to slowly enjoy and appreciate as much as possible. And, to give the word it's just due, I should spell it in the proper European way, savour. Now I like it even more.

In psychology, savouring (yep, keeping the British spelling, spell-check be damned) refers to intentionally focusing on the details and positive aspects of the experience. It's an effective way to reduce stress and increase happiness and the quality of life. Enjoying and appreciating the experience distracts us from lamenting about what we don't have. And yes, the conversation has moved beyond food.

As we savour, we focus on the details of the little things. The turn of the smile, the sparkle in her eyes when she laughs, the smell of her hair, and the softness as you hold her hand. Do you see where this can go? Focus on sensations: the sounds of children laughing, the smell of the ocean breeze, the feel of the morning sun on a spring day, and seeing the shades of color at sunset over the lake. Just writing about savouring and how it can contribute to the way we think, feel, and live life provides a clear understanding of how it can contribute to our well-being.

216

There is another life process that works well with savouring, almost picking up where savouring leaves off, and that's the important emotion of gratitude. Human nature is to dwell on the negative in life. This tendency, called negative bias, is rooted in our evolutionary genealogy when, to stay alive, our ancestors always had to focus on the bad things that could happen. In today's world, it brings a propensity to focus on problems, annoyances, and injustices in our lives which leaves little room for focusing on the positive. The good news is that saber-toothed tigers are extinct. Better news, there is something we can do to increase our ability to practice gratitude.

With effort, we can change negative thought patterns. Research, along with common sense, shows us that the effort's well worth it. Feeling grateful can have a powerfully positive effect on our lives. Cultivating gratitude is not about ignoring painful feelings or dismissing challenges. It's about the simple act of focusing daily on the positive in life, finding room for the good stuff.

Research by Jeffrey Froh, associate professor of psychology at Hofstra University, found that people who feel grateful are more optimistic, report more social satisfaction, experience less envy, have less anxiety and depression, sleep better, do better in school and at work, feel better, derive more satisfaction in life, have better relationships, and live a better life. The list went on, but we get the point. Having gratitude is a good thing.

Research also shows that we can develop gratitude through practice, and the more we practice, the better we are at it. Love it. Here are some thoughts on how to practice gratitude; not all will sound appealing, so pick a few and try them out. I'm hoping you will be grateful you did.

- Journal. Some would call it gratitude journaling, but it doesn't need a name. Write down some thoughts each night. What are you grateful for? What are the few good things that crossed your path during the day?

- Start your day with gratitude. Think about things you are grateful for over coffee. Or write a few down and stick the note in your pocket, or shoe, or wherever. Take a look during the day if you need a boost.

- Write and send thank-you notes. Do you want to knock someone's socks off? Go old school and send them a note. A bit less sock-knocking, share the sentiment in an email.

- Pray. Or call it meditation. Spend a few minutes just thinking about or thanking your God for what you are grateful for. Cover the big items such as family, friends, health, and life. But grab a couple of small ones from the day—the blue sky, birds singing, the smile you gave, or the door you opened. This can be so calming.

- Mental subtraction. Imagine life if that positive thing or person was not there or didn't happen. Kinda *It's a Wonderful Life* process.

- Don't go it alone. Have a gratitude buddy, someone you trust can share the experience.

- Be mindful if or when your thoughts and language start to turn negative.

- Don't dwell on the past or overthink the future.

- Pause when you find a nugget of goodness and tell yourself, This is good.

- Start small, pick a couple of ideas, and practice. You don't have to go full Pollyanna to start. Although there is nothing wrong with being Pollyannaish, regardless of what my wife thinks.

Enjoy your life and do your thing. Enjoy it to the fullest through savouring and gratitude. In the words of Hans Christian Andersen, "Enjoy your life. There is plenty of time to be dead." Apparently, the author of 156 children's fairy tales had a bit of stoic sarcasm in his personality.

There we have it. Ten pillars that will help in our quest to be happy, healthy and lengthen our health span. Enjoy your journey.

Interestingly, just as I finished this conversation, I ran across a novel titled *Twelve Pillars* written by Jim Rohn and Chris Widener. The name comes from one of the stories in the book. It contains fundamental principles for a successful plan in life. A couple of our principles overlapped—relationships and lifelong learning. They included one that may be of interest to us: leaving a legacy. I may want to read the book to learn more.

The One Thing That Could Change Everything

Wow, that conversation title would be considered click-bait if we were online. And maybe it's a bit intentional on my part. Yes, I do think the strength of a title has merit.

What's this claim of such power and strength that promises to change someone's aging experience? The one thing that supersedes all else and might change lives for the better? Optimism.

I can envision my wife rolling her eyes at the exact moment she read this. The kind of eye roll that's so pronounced it's nearly audible, is accompanied by a head shake and maybe a lip smack. "Really," she would say. "That's the big reveal?"

A little insight about my wife would help you at this moment. She claims to be a realist, which is an optimistic way of saying she is a pessimist. That glass half full or half empty, that whole thing. It's not unusual for us to see the same situation but have very different points of view. There are times when I think she has no glass, as mine sits at least half full.

In full transparency, I'm writing this conversation with a strong bias toward optimism. This quote from Winston Churchill nicely summarizes my slant on the topic. Churchill, in his infinite wisdom, said, "A pessimist sees difficulty in every opportunity. An optimist sees the opportunity in every difficulty." Can I just say that I understand?

My wife might not be alone in her reaction or view of life. To her and all of those like her, I simply ask you to stay with me as I present my case. Be optimistic and open-minded. (Do you see me slipping that in right there?) And maybe, just maybe, we can move closer to consensus or at least acknowledge each other's point of view.

A Boston University School of Medicine and Harvard School of Public Health study published in 2019 suggests that people who tend to be optimistic are more likely to live to be 85 years old or older. "The finding is independent of other longevity factors such as socioeconomic status, health conditions, social integration, and other health behaviors" said Clinical Research Psychologist Lewina Lee, who headed the study.

Researchers knew from previous studies that optimistic individuals tend to have a reduced risk of depression, heart disease, and other chronic diseases. The study, which included 69,744 women and 1,429 men (interesting ratio?), found that optimism demonstrated, on average, 11 percent to15 percent longer life span, and greater odds of reaching the age of 85 when compared to the least optimistic group.

A more recent study conducted by the Harvard T.H. Chan School of Public Health confirmed the older findings as they were focused on positive psychological factors, like optimism, as possible pathways for promoting health and longevity. They found that 25 percent of the most optimistic people had a 5.4 percent longer life span, equating to 4.4 years, and a 10 percent greater likelihood of living to and beyond the age of 90.

But why? Why do glass-half-full people live longer? Maybe the short answer is because they want to. The longer answer is that life is easier and generally more enjoyable if you're an optimist. Research shows that optimists enjoy many health and lifestyle benefits, including greater achievement, better health, a sense of persistence toward goals, greater emotional health, lower reaction to stress, and a greater sense of purpose. Optimists tend to live happier lives.

Clinical psychologist Natalie Dattilo, PhD, from Brigham and Women's Hospital in Boston, says even if it doesn't come naturally, optimism can be learned. It's a matter of changing your mindset. Dr. Dattilo works to expand a patient's point of view to allow for a broader look at life. Challenges viewed up close, under a microscope, tend to look much bigger, in some cases bigger than they need to be. She adds optimism isn't the absence of depression, sadness, or stress, it's the resilience to deal with the situation. Optimism plays a large role in our ability to bounce back, even in times of setbacks. To be able to see a better, more positive outcome and provide certain motivation in which to achieve that outcome.

Because optimism is modifiable, characteristics can be changed with interventions such as writing, exercise, and therapy, all with the goal of improved health and more positive well-being.

I may not have convinced anyone of the merits of optimism, but speaking as a dyed-in-the-wool optimist, let me share this. When I wake up in the morning, I always think that today can be a good day, and I plan to do everything in my power to make that happen. In many ways, it almost becomes a self-fulfilling prophecy. Some days I'm wrong, but many days I'm right. It seems to work for me.

Mark Twain said, "It is better to be an optimist who is sometimes wrong than a pessimist who is always right."

Learned optimism is a concept that emerged out of a relatively young branch of psychology known as positive psychology. It was introduced by Martin Seligman, PhD, who is considered one of the founders of the positive psychology movement.

Traditional psychology tends to look for problems and focus on a fix. (It's usually your parents' fault, or so it seems.) Positive psychology focuses on what's good and makes it better. The belief is optimism can lead to happier, healthier, and longer lives.

I was intrigued, but I needed to know if Dr. Seligman was legit or just some feel-good doctor. It turns out he is legit, very legit. He attended Princeton, and earned a doctorate from the University of Pennsylvania, was an assistant professor at Cornell before he returned to Penn as a professor and was elected to be the President of the American Psychological Association in 1996 by the largest margin in the organization's history at that time. He is the 13th most cited psychologist in psych textbooks. I think he is believable, so I'm ready to read what he has to say.

According to Dr. Seligman, the process of learned optimism is an important way to help people maximize their mental health and live better lives—an objective that would apply to people of all ages. Seligman goes on to say, "Anyone can learn the skills to be more optimistic. It can be a route to finding your purpose in life. With a firm belief in a positive future, you often find yourself focused on more meaningful activities."

Here are some of the ways he suggests to increase optimism:

1. First, don't force it. Behavior modification takes practice to become second nature. It can almost feel uncomfortable at first.

2. Remember that we all fail at times. You are not alone.

3. View failure differently. As Albert Einstein said, "Failure is simply another way of learning."

4. Change perspective. Problems can become opportunities.

5. Zoom out. How much will this really matter five years from now, or maybe even five days from now?

6. Choose your own version of optimism. Everything doesn't have to be rosy, just choose to move more toward the middle on the optimism scale.

7. Question your pessimistic thoughts. Thoughts are not facts, pauses, and questions.

8. Surround yourself with optimistic people.

9. Think about what advice you would give your best friend. Then, be your best friend. (I love this concept.)

In yet another study done in 2019 by the Johns Hopkins Bloomberg School of Public Health, it's reported that optimistic participants had a 24 percent increased likelihood of maintaining a healthy aging lifestyle. Not only does optimism have a direct effect on health, happiness, and longevity, it also has a positive effect on our motivation to make positive lifestyle choices that can lead to health, happiness, and longevity. Optimism for the win.

Not so fast, says my wife, drinking her coffee just past the half-empty point, although it looked half-full to me. A little explanation could be helpful. I always like to say, don't believe me, I'm just quoting the experts. That goes over well as I'm sure you can imagine.

The experts say that focusing on avoiding failure or negative outcomes can have a negative impact on motivation. This can be a problem for people who are avoidance motivated by nature, people who lack motivation or look for reasons not to move forward.

Optimists, on the other hand, expect to succeed, which reduces the negative effects of lack of motivation.

Is it possible to be too optimistic? Well, yes, it is, apparently. Optimism can be too extreme when people underestimate potential threats or take high risks in hopeless endeavors such as gambling.

I have been accused of being a Pollyanna in my life, which as it turns out, may not be quite as bad as my accuser would have thought. The noun Pollyanna is used to describe someone characterized as blindly optimistic. It comes from the 1913 novel *Pollyanna* by American author Eleanor Porter. The book is considered a children's classic and the success led to a sequel called *Pollyanna Grows Up*, published in 1915. Eleven more books followed in the series, which came to be known as the *Glad Books*.

In the books, Pollyanna and her father would play the "Glad Game" as a method of coping with the difficulties and sorrows of everyday life. The story follows the title character, Pollyanna Whittier, an 11-year-old who, after her mother dies, goes to live in the fictional town of Beldingsville, Vermont, with her grouchy aunt.

The Glad Game she and her father played centered around the idea to find something to be glad about in every situation. Her glad spirit and sunny personality transform the town into a pleasant place to live. Wow, people making people happy; can we even imagine?

Eventually, Pollyanna's robust optimism is tested when she is struck by a car and loses the use of her legs. Her spirits plummet, not able to find anything to be glad about. The townspeople rally and return the positive spirit she had spread.

Pollyanna was glad that she still had her legs and hoped that someday she could use them to walk again. She did.

One quote from the book was borrowed from Abe Lincoln and modified to fit the story, "When you look for the bad, expecting it, you will surely get it." I look forward to the next time I will be honored with the name Pollyanna.

***

As it turns out, my wife is not the only one in the family with an aversion toward optimism. My daughter developed a strong streak of pessimism in high school. Genetics? It would rear its ugly head around test time, a natural occurrence, many might say. When we asked, "How do you feel about the test?" She would always reply, "I'm going to fail." Every. Single. Time.

In the follow-up discussion, we would discover she got an A, or on a rare occasion, a B. Did I mention my daughter is very intelligent, like her mother? Genetics again?

This went on through high school and followed her to college until once, in her senior year, she actually failed a test. "See, I told you I would fail." Yes, after seven years and hundreds of times telling us, she finally did. I'm reminded of Mark Twain's quote, "I have known many troubles, some of which actually happened."

I think about my daughter's life over the past seven years. The hundreds of tests and thousands of hours of anxiety all justified by one test. If I could just go back in time, I would play the Glad Game with her.

Can you do something for me? (Not you, Tiny. [Tiny is my daughter's nickname. She is five foot nine now, but she will always be our Tiny.]) The rest of the readers, please join in. When you wake up tomorrow, tell yourself it's going to be a good day, and then do everything you can to make it happen. Better idea, don't do it for me, do it for yourself. Happy optimism, and enjoy your day.

WWDPNGD

Do you remember the WWJD bracelets popular in the 90s? I didn't own one, but I liked the concept. Religious or not, you have to agree that Jesus was a pretty moral guy making good decisions for all the right reasons. Many would consider him the expert in morality. The bracelet would remind us to make good decisions by asking ourselves, what would Jesus do?

As it turns out, the thought process behind the bracelet has a long and storied history. You can certainly find roots for the idea in the Bible, but the first secular writing of an official introduction can be traced back to the early 1400s when Thomas à Kempis wrote *Imitatio Christi* (*The Imitation of Christ*), a Christian devotional book.

Four hundred years later, pulpit-pounding preacher Charles Spurgeon peppered one of his sermons with the phrase in 1881 in London. The crowd went wild, but no bracelets yet.

It was Reverend Charles Sheldon who introduced it to a wider audience. In 1890, Reverend Sheldon was the leader of the Central Congregational Church of Topeka, Kansas. He had grown frustrated with the light attendance at the Sunday evening service, so he started to present a moral dilemma and ended with the cliffhanger, "What would Jesus do?" Attendance surged. Reverend Sheldon went on to write a book in 1896 titled *In His Steps*, which carried the same theme. It became an international best seller. Still no bracelets.

Then 100 years later, Janie Tinklenberg, a youth leader at the Calvary Reformed Church in Holland, Michigan, had an idea. After reading Reverend Sheldon's book, she decided to update the moral decision process with the WWJD acronym, which she put on a bracelet. Then came T-shirts, bumper stickers, coffee mugs, and anything else that could be printed with WWJD.

The micro story for me in all of this is that when making important decisions, turn to the experts. What would the experts do? I use this philosophy in a number of areas in my life. Food, for instance. Certainly not at the same level as a moral dilemma, and no, I don't think, WWJD? In a restaurant, for example, I ask servers, "What's your favorite item on the menu?" Recently I had a vegan server: I asked, "What's the most popular dish?" I loved the occasion when I narrowed the options down to three and the server said, "I will surprise you." The breakfast brisket was fantastic, not the healthiest option on the menu, but yummy. She made a wise choice. And she made that choice because she knows. She works there. She was the expert.

Two years ago, I used the same decision process in a conversation with my primary care physician. I have struggled with high cholesterol all my life, or at least as long as I bothered to have it checked. I didn't want to start taking a statin despite the fact it's the most prescribed drug category in the world. But it can have side effects and is controversial—a topic for another day.

For the six months leading up to my blood test and appointment, I did everything I could to naturally lower my LDL (low-density lipoprotein); I really worked hard at it. My numbers did improve, but not enough. During the discussion about cholesterol and the next steps, my doctor, the expert in the room, provided the following advice: "Garry," he said, in his calm but firm voice, "you have done everything you can do to lower your cholesterol, and I applaud you. Clearly, your levels are a result of familial hypercholesterolemia, which is caused by inherited changes (mutations) in LDLR, APOB, and PCSK9 genes. My recommendation for you is to try 20 milligrams of a statin. If that doesn't work for you, we can reevaluate the situation." He had my attention at "familial," but it was his next line that sealed the deal, "I have a similar situation, and I take 20 milligrams of a statin." Yep, if it's good enough for the expert, in this case, Dr. Sam, it's good enough for me.

I took 20 milligrams of the statin daily for one year, and sure enough, my cholesterol levels are very good. However, given my need to push the envelope, some may refer to this as being stubborn, I reduced my statin to 10 milligrams, still maintaining a healthy lifestyle and going back for a blood test and doctor visit in six months. This time, we will be measuring cholesterol and ApoB (Apolipoprotein B). ApoB is a structural protein found in all potentially atherogenic (plaque-forming) particles, possibly a better indicator of cardiovascular health than cholesterol alone. However, in the end, I will listen to the expert, Dr Sam.

Speaking of experts, I thought it would be interesting to understand what longevity experts do to increase their health span. I mean, they are the ones studying this stuff every day. What can we learn from their personal choices? We'll be looking at a few of the longevity experts that I follow which will also explain the acronym for this conversation, WWDPNGD.

The D in the acronym above stands for David Sinclair, MD: professor of genetics at Harvard Medical School and a leading researcher in the field of longevity. *Time* magazine in 2014 named him "one of the most influential people in the world."

The P stands for Peter Attia, MD: Stanford-trained physician, best-selling author, big-time podcaster, and founder of Early Medical, a medical practice that applies medicine 3.0 with the goal of lengthening the health span of patients.

The N stands for Nir Barziliai, MD: professor of medicine and genetics at Albert Einstein College of Medicine, founding director of the Institute of Aging Research, the NIH's Nathan Shock Center of Excellence in the Basic Biology of Aging, and the Paul F. Glenn Center for the Biology of Human Aging Research at Albert Einstein College of Medicine. On a personal note, my son is currently a second-year medical student at Albert Einstein College of Medicine. He is still enjoying his life of "first best days ever."

These guys can truly be considered experts in aging, so who better to understand what they do personally for their health and extension of health span? I was excited to do this research, understand it, and possibly adjust my life accordingly. Oh yeah, so the G in the acronym is me- Garry. Not an expert, just an enthusiastic old guy wanting to live a happy, healthy, and long life.

We need a huge disclaimer here. The following is not medical advice. It's simply my research of information that's available to the public regarding the lifestyle and supplements these experts take. It's very likely that some of the information is incomplete or has even changed. As the experts themselves would tell you, we are all different, and medicine and supplements are very personal. Any thoughts of taking a supplement or any change to lifestyle or medication must be discussed with your personal physician. Okay, with that out of the way, let's dive in.

The focus of this discussion will be on supplements. Because as you can imagine, these experts do everything they can to live a healthy lifestyle. Think about what that means to you and ramp it up five times: healthy sleep patterns, daily exercise, a Mediterranean-influenced diet leaning toward vegan (although Dr. Barzilai's favorite meal is the occasional chicken paprikash, which he was happy to learn didn't spike his glucose levels but may spike yours), and intermittent fasting. As it turns out, it is not just what we eat, but also when we eat that can influence our health.

With healthy living as a starting point, each of the doctors takes supplements. Not exactly the same ones, but there are many product overlaps. These are presented alphabetically with a brief explanation of each. As a reminder, these supplements were chosen by them to meet very personalized health plans. What works for them may or may not work for us. However, with that said, it's worth understanding and warrants further exploration on our part. The brevity of the explanation may also leave out important information that may be relevant, so again, I encourage additional research and discussion with your medical professional.

- Alpha-lipoic acid (ALA) is found in some foods and can be produced naturally in the mitochondria, which plays an essential role in converting nutrients into energy. ALA may reduce markers of inflammation, improve cholesterol and triglyceride levels, support glucose levels, and improve body composition.

- Baby aspirin is an old-time favorite. Baby aspirin may lower the risk of heart attack and stroke. This is currently under debate, and the benefit-risk ratio may depend on age and current cardiovascular condition.

- Vitamin B12: Humans cannot produce B12 naturally, so it must be absorbed through diet or supplements. Vitamin B12 is needed for producing red blood cells, ensuring that the brain and nervous system work effectively, and is a critical vitamin that aids in energy production and muscle repair.

- Coenzyme Q10 (CoQ10) is an enzyme synthesized naturally by the body and found in almost every cell. It works to stimulate mitochondria to help our body convert food into energy efficiently. CoQ10 also works as an antioxidant to help prevent cell damage.

- Curcumin is a biologically active polyphenolic compound found in turmeric. It has antioxidant and anti-inflammatory properties that can help to lower the risk of heart disease, Alzheimer's, metabolic syndrome, arthritis, anxiety and depression, cancer, and other degenerative diseases.

- Vitamin D3 is essential for bone health, muscle strength, and overall health. The body can only absorb calcium when vitamin D is present. Vitamin D works to reduce inflammation; it's an antioxidant with neuroprotective properties that support the immune system, muscle function, and brain cell activity. More sun, salmon, and sardines into your life.

- Athletic Greens (AG1) is a brand-name comprehensive nutrition and gut health support supplement containing 75 vitamins and minerals and whole food-sourced nutrients. One scoop in a glass of water helps to support gut health and the immune system, boosts energy, and helps support body recovery. Basically, a bunch of good-for-you stuff in a glass of water.

- Lithium has been shown to increase autophagy, enhance the generation of pluripotent cells, demonstrate its epigenetic effects, and improve neurogenesis and the formation of new neurons.

235

- Vitamin K2 is gaining recognition for its positive effects on blood clotting, heart health, and bone health. This micronutrient can be found in green leafy vegetables.

- Magnesium is an indispensable mineral for the body to function properly. Magnesium can help to reduce inflammation, manage blood pressure, lower the risk of heart disease, lower the risk of neurodegenerative disease, lower the risk of osteoporosis, and even lower the risk of some cancers. Magnesium can also provide energy that can help people deal with stress.

- Metformin is often the first line of treatment for type 2 diabetes. Metformin manages liver glucose production and promotes insulin secretion. Studies also suggest that it may play a role in improving cognition, lowering the occurrence of cardiovascular events, and reducing all-cause mortality.

- Methylfolate, also known as L-methylfolate, is an active natural form of vitamin B9. Methylfolate supports brain function and a healthy mood by helping your body produce the neurotransmitters serotonin, dopamine, and norephedrine. It also may reduce the risk of heart disease and reduce some cancers. Interestingly to note, methylfolate is the only form of folate that can cross the blood-brain barrier, which seems like that would be a big deal in supporting brain function.

- N-acetylcysteine (NAC) helps to replenish glutathione, arguably your most powerful antioxidant. By regulating glutamate levels in the brain, NAC may alleviate symptoms of some mental health conditions. NAC's antioxidant and expectorant can improve lung function by decreasing inflammation and breaking up mucus.

- Nicotinamide mononucleotide (NMN) is needed to make NAD+, which is a very important substance for our cells. It provides energy and is a cofactor for proteins to repair and maintain our epigenome and DNA. Various studies show that NMN has beneficial effects on aging diseases and their symptoms, including reducing inflammation, improving mitochondria function, and improving bone health and vascular health.

- Omega-3 fatty acid is most often found in fish oil. It works to keep your heart healthy by improving cholesterol levels and may also help maintain stable blood glucose levels.

- Quercetin is an abundant flavonoid found in many fruits and vegetables. Interest in quercetin stems from its possible influence on cardiovascular disease and high cholesterol.

- Rapamycin is an immunosuppressant that may have antiaging effects. Rapamycin inhibits the activity of mTOR, a signaling pathway involved in regulating stress, growth, and metabolism. Rapamycin was found on Easter Island in 1972. The "rapa" part of its name is a nod to the Rapa Nui monoliths.

- Resveratrol, a polyphenol, has garnered attention for its potential effects on aging. Resveratrol has an influence on metabolic syndrome, a group of conditions that include hypertension, obesity, high triglycerides, and impaired fasting glucose. Break out the red wine. May I suggest a Cannonau di Sardegna (local name for grenache), a red from the Blue Zone of Sardinia? It's said to be the healthiest wine in the world, with up to three times the concentration of flavonoids (antioxidants).

- Selenium is a mineral that can help to support metabolism, the immune system, and thyroid function. Selenium is a powerful antioxidant that helps to protect cells from damage caused by oxidative stress. It's thought to help keep your heart healthy, lower the risk of certain cancers, and slow mental decline.

- Spermidine: Spermidine is an aliphatic polyamine that helps to synchronize an array of biological processes and induce autophagy through the TOR Kinase pathway. Thus, cells reuse old or damaged organelle to achieve cellular renewal, thus its antiaging benefits. It also protects hair health.

- Statins (HMG-CoA reductase inhibitors) are a class of lipid-lowering medications that reduce illness and mortality for those who are at high risk for cardiovascular disease. They are the most common cholesterol-lowering drug available.

There you have it, a sampling of supplements used by experts in the human longevity industry. Medical doctors, researchers, and professors ingest these supplements in an effort to live a longer, healthier life.

There is no substitute for learning from the experts who are active in their field. They spent years in the field to gain the foundation that they now apply on a daily basis. And when they apply their knowledge to their own health, it's reasonable to take notice. So I have.

The experts have influenced my lifestyle over the past couple of years. Although I have not jumped in fully, (I'm averse to taking pills) I have adapted to the following small changes in my life.

- Statins: You already heard my story.

- Curcumin: I take 750 milligrams per day with food

- Nutrition: I follow a modified Mediterranean diet. I do enjoy a steak on special occasions.

- Intermittent fasting, cheater style: I limit my calorie intake to an eight-hour window. Not as hard to do as I thought.

- Cold shower: We haven't talked about it, but according to research, my painful three minutes of cold water at the end of my shower is healthy for many reasons. (This is legit. Read about it, try it, you won't love it.)

- AG1: I drink 12 ounces every morning. This stuff looks, smells, and tastes like the water run-off from a cleansed lawn mower. It's packed with good stuff that we need, so I look forward to drinking it first thing every morning because it makes me feel as though I'm starting the day off in a healthy way. And what do they say, "Own the morning, win the day." Not sure who says it, but it sounds like someone should.

- Metformin: Currently one of the leading drugs and/ or supplements that may increase longevity. I have a prescription from my doctor, but I have not yet filled it.

- Exercise: I walk with the dog daily and spend 45 minutes for weight training five days a week.

And that's it. Is it working? I honestly don't know. I sleep well, feel well, rarely get sick, and have lots of energy. The answer may be yes. But I have never been this age before. Therefore, I am not exactly sure how good I should feel. I will continue to watch the experts, monitor my results, and work toward the best possible outcome.

CONVERSATION 31

Living on Purpose

Do you know a person that seems to do life well? Everything just seems to fall in place. Problems have a way of working out. They always show up on time, looking good, with some interesting story to share, but not until after hearing news about your day. Yes, that person. We can set aside our envy because they are so fun to be around. Are they lucky? Well, maybe as long as we buy into the definition of luck that suggests that it happens when preparation meets opportunity. I think this person lives intentionally. They make things happen, more than letting things happen to them. How do they do it? Maybe they live a balanced life.

A recent study supports the idea that maintaining life balance is not only essential for your health and happiness, but it can be a tremendous boost to your productivity and success in life. When you take steps to find balance in your life, you have a far greater ability to focus your attention on goals and take productive action to move forward in life in a meaningful way. "Doing Life Well."

A couple of quick disclaimers before we move forward on this very important topic.

You may be thinking, what does this have to do with aging? A fair question, and yes, this topic has relevance for people of any age, maybe even mentoring moment for my kids. (Love you guys.) However, this has a strong application for us as we age as you will soon see.

The other disclaimer is the noticeable overlap with the 10 pillars conversation. But there is an important difference. The pillar strategy is narrowly focused on happiness, health, and longevity over a long period of time. Life balance is a process that can have an immediate effect on our daily lives. But the good news is, balancing the dimensions in our lives can, in fact, have positive long-term effects as well. When you think about it, life is simply made up of living one day followed by the next. Yes, balance can help with living a better life.

When life gets busy, it's easy to find ourselves off balance, not paying attention to certain important dimensions. Strangely the same can happen when life gets less busy, as in retirement. Certain dimensions in life go away and priorities change. If we don't manage the transition, we can find ourselves out of balance and with unhealthy patterns. A life out of balance can feel like a constant battle.

What is balance, you may be asking? It's understanding which dimensions in life are important to you, then dedicating the time, energy, and resources to make each dimension healthy and synergistic with the rest. It's living intentionally, realizing that life isn't stable but in constant motion. Balance is not a destination but something we must constantly work on, kinda like a juggling act, or as Albert Einstein once said, "Life is like riding a bike. To keep balance, you must keep moving."

How do you know if your life is out of balance? Here are some symptoms.

- Can't find time to do things you know need to be done

- Not happy

- Don't feel well

- Feelings of anxiety or depression

- Overwhelmed or burned out

- You want a better life

Solution: If you don't like your life, change the way you live. Seek a new balance, add, delete, or adjust the balance between dimensions to maximize living. Maybe a bit oversimplified, but let's keep it that way-simple.

The first step in the process is to determine the dimensions in your life. Key values and priorities that are important to you. Many are common to us all and will change throughout our lives. By way of example, let me share a list of dimensions from a hypothetical person we will call Garry, a semiretired male who is spending a great deal of time writing a book. "His" dimensions are

- Family

- Physical Health

- Purpose

- Intellectual stimulation and continuous learning

- Spiritual well-being

- Emotional/mental health

- Social life

- Financial health and occupation

- Activities and interests

- Other (like getting stuff done)

Over time, this list has changed, particularly in order of priority. Not surprisingly, family has always been at the top of the list, and despite not spending as much time with the kids, who are grown and gone, family will always be my top priority. (Oh, I mean "his" top priority.)

Physical health has jumped up a few places now that I have more time and a better understanding of its importance. I wish I would have taken action sooner.

Financial health has moved down the list as I'm at a "semi-retired" point in my life and don't need to spend the time and effort in career chasing.

Mental health may seem a bit low on the list, not that it's not important, but it's receiving the "ride-along" benefit of many of my other priorities. Much of what's needed to keep my emotional and mental health strong is covered in my dimensions and lifestyle choices, including physical health, purpose, intellectual stimulation, spiritual well-being, and social life. This provides an important point—the interplay between the dimensions and the need to find balance between them.

In her book *Why Has Nobody Told Me This Before*, Dr. Julie Smith reminds us, "Everything we do and don't do influences our mood. The longer you avoid exercise, the more you feel lethargic, and your mental health suffers. The constant feedback between the brain, the body, and your environment will greatly affect how we feel both physically and emotionally."

It happens. Imbalance happens to all of us because life is constantly changing. Balance helps the process of holding life together during those times of change.

A tool commonly used by professional life coaches is the wheel of life (or life wheel). It can help to identify areas in your life that need to come into balance, sometimes more, sometimes less. It helps to zoom out and take a helicopter view, a top-down approach to bring things back into balance.

Here is a six-step process that may help:

1. Understand your dimensions. Are they still the same, or has a life transition occurred requiring an evaluation?

2. Prioritize your dimensions. What's really important for you to move forward with your life?

3. Integrate aspects of your life rather than have dimensions always competing for your time.

4. Evaluate the past week or month, some period of time that allows an honest assessment of how well you did for each dimension. Be honest; what's suffering?

5. Develop an improvement plan. Only you can make it better.

6. Bonus: Don't worry about balance; just be aware of the need for it. Focus on living a good life, one that allows you to move forward in a positive way. Balance is often the result.

Finding balance is an ongoing process. It's not a finite goal; it's a constant journey. Enjoy your day, and balance for tomorrow.

CONVERSATION 32

The Phone Call

It was a beautiful August day. I was on the lake with my kids in the pontoon boat, the perfect floating playpen. We were enjoying life so much that I didn't even realize I didn't have my mobile phone. But I was on the lake with the kids, time to relax. I didn't need a phone, or so I thought.

After a few hours of fun and freedom, we went home to find my wife greeting us on the dock, which was the first sign that something was not right. "You didn't take your phone," she said sternly. No, I forgot it. "Your Dad has been trying to reach you." The second sign. "What did he want," I asked. "You really need to call him." And then I knew.

I called my dad to learn the news. My mom had passed away. She had spent her last four years in a nursing home suffering from the ill effects of advanced Parkinson's disease and dementia. For the first three years, she would ask every day, "When am I going home?" We knew the answer but always skirted the question, maybe not the best way to handle the situation.

Her last year was, in a word, horrible. She was basically in a coma, although never medically diagnosed as such. She was in a sleep state 24/7 and couldn't be woken. All bodily functions were handled through tubes.

On a rare occasion, she would join the conversation. Only two or three sentences and then she would fade back into her world, a world that protected her from the reality of what she was living. Her comments were well thought out and reflected the mom we all knew and loved, sometimes even flavored with her witty sarcasm. We wished for more.

The call was not a surprise. We had been expecting it for years. It was the type of call that could be described as a blessing, she is in a better place. And whatever your spiritual belief, it would be hard to disagree.

This is the call we all receive in our life, or maybe we're the ones making it, which in some cases may actually be more difficult. It's the call that generates emotions of love, sadness, and anxiety. I should have been there, but what could I have done? She was such a big part of my life. I love my mom.

She loved the movie *Forrest Gump*, especially the sage and famous line Forrest says, "My momma always said, 'Life was like a box of chocolates; you never know what you're gonna get.'" During another touching scene, Forrest recalls, "Momma always said that 'dyin' was part of life.'" Mrs. Gump was a smart woman. People don't like thinking about death. We mourn the deceased and don't talk about the deaths of the future. Certainly not our own death, but maybe we should.

Tim McGraw released his album *Live Like You Were Dying* in June 2004, and the title song went gold. As the title would indicate he promotes the idea to live like we were dying. News flash- we are.

> Someday I hope you get a chance
> To live like you were dying
> Like tomorrow was a gift

Tim McGraw certainly didn't own the corner of songs touching the theme of death. I can literally visualize ol' Blue Eyes, Frank Sinatra, belting out his classic hit, "My Way," which we all want to be played during our eulogy.

> The record shows
> I took the blows
> And did it my way.

We are fond of these songs about death. Not because they are about dying; they are about living. Death teaches us *how to live*. Sinatra would be the first to tell us you only go around once, but if you play your cards right, once is enough.

Steve Jobs delivered the commencement speech at Stanford in 2005, arguably the greatest commencement speech ever, and yes I quote from it often. During the speech he said a few things about death. Having faced his own mortality in dealing with pancreatic cancer, he knew a few things about the topic. An informal expert, if you will. He announced to the crowd of students, facility, and family, all on the cusp of launching the next phase of their young lives, that "death is very likely the single best invention of life" Whhaaattt? This is a crowd celebrating the achievements of smart 21-year-olds about to enter a new and very exciting phase in their lives, and he is talking about the benefits of death. It didn't seem to make sense . . . until it did.

He went on to say, "Your time is limited, so don't waste it living someone else's life." He followed up with a life-altering question, "If today were the last day of your life, would you want to do what you are about to do today?" Wow!

Do you see a common theme? Death is all about how to live a better, more fulfilling life. We have two lives in this world. One begins the day we are born; the second begins when we realize that someday we're going to die. Jobs included another line in his speech. "If you live each day as if it were your last, someday you'll certainly be right."

***

The second call was very different. After my mom passed, we thought my dad would soon follow, as often happens with older couples who had spent many years together. He didn't. He went on to live another 13 years, most of those in an independent senior community. His small, one-bedroom apartment was a shrine to my mom, with over 50 photos of her and the two of them together celebrating life. Every table and each inch of wall space was part of the celebration. She was not gone; she was still very much a part of his life. Memories are wonderful in that way.

My dad was 92 when he moved to Wisconsin to live with my sister. God bless her. He had never lived outside of Michigan and, now at 92, he became a Cheesehead." I don't think he knew or cared. During Dad's first week living with my sister, friends from her church visited. My dad was proudly introducing his family to his new friends using a picture on the table close to him, a picture that traveled with him from Michigan and was always in close proximity.

"This is my son Donald Jr. He lives in California. This is my other son, Garry. He is my favorite." (I added that part.) "This is my daughter, Patty. She passed away. He may have forgotten that Patty was sitting next to him holding his hand. That's okay, we forget things sometimes. My sister was laughing as she told me the story, so I knew it was okay to ask if he happened to mention how she died. He hadn't and she laughed again.

My dad did well for a year but then needed more care so moved him to the local nursing home. In small-town Wisconsin, everyone is family so it was good.

Each time I visited, I would cry in my car as I was leaving, thinking this may have been the last time I saw my dad.

Then I got the call. My sister said my dad was not doing well. I jumped in my car for what was to be my last eight-hour drive to see him. It was a difficult drive in many ways, but one that helped in my grieving process. I spent eight wonderful hours reliving memories of time together with my dad and with my family. At times, I needed to stop when the tears made it difficult to drive. But I remembered so many wonderful times: Sunday dinners, TV dinners, and summer barbecues. We liked to eat. Holidays were always special with my dad decorating the house and wearing his red vest during gift giving. And his love for my mom.

I arrived at the nursing home hoping to have one more conversation with my dad to tell him how much he meant to me and that I loved him. I said the words, I hope he heard me.

*　*　*

My sister and I would spend the day with my dad and then go home for dinner, returning the next morning to do it again.

On that night, July 5, just 21 days before his 95th birthday, I decided to go back after dinner. I don't know if God told me to go, or if God told my dad that I was there. My dad decided to leave that night as I held his hand, listening to Christmas music in the middle of the summer. Christmas music made him happy.

I wrote a eulogy that reflected his life. Here's an excerpt.

My dad decided to go to heaven. He was 95. I had the opportunity to watch him take his last peaceful breath on earth at 10:10 p.m. on Sunday, July 5.

1 Corinthians 13:13
"And now these three things remain: faith, hope, and love. But the greatest of these is Love."

Love is the word that best describes my dad's life. He had a great love for his faith, family, friends, and food. He lived a wonderful life in his pursuit of each.

I will always cherish the memories of his love and thank him for passing on many of the same values I enjoy in my life.

When choosing a headstone for my mother 13 years ago, he selected one with both of their names. When asked what he would like it to say, he didn't hesitate: Love Forever.

My dad is with my mom in heaven now. I picture them on the front porch of a small white house with a sidewalk out front where friends can pass by. They are enjoying the most tender pork chops, the freshest strawberry shortcake, and the sweetest iced tea.

Yes, they are happy. Love Forever.

* * *

In Hindu families, relatives and friends come together to support the family in an elaborate thirteen-day mourning ritual. My dad passed during our nation's struggle with COVID- 19. Our gathering was small: my sister, brother, me, and my wife and kids.

One Christmas, I gave my dad a book that featured twelve important questions to ask your dad before he is gone. Questions I am sure can be found in many books about parental relationships. You may own one.

1. What were you most proud of?

2. Why did you choose your career?

3. Who was influential in your life?

4. What did you admire most about your father?

5. What was your biggest life lesson?

6. Is there anything you regret in life?

7. How would your father describe you?

8. What mistake taught you most about life?

9. What world event had the most impact on you?

10. What did you enjoy most about being a father?

11. What was the hardest moment as a father?

12. What's the one story that I don't know?

And the question I would have asked: If you lived your life over, what, if anything, would you have changed?

I cried as I read the book. I was heartbroken that I couldn't answer the questions. I didn't know my dad as well as I thought. Although I think I know the answer to my add-on question. His answer would have been no, he wouldn't have changed a thing.

In 2021, sixteen years after Steve Jobs' speech at Stanford, Jobs' widow, Laurene Powell Jobs, delivered the commencement speech to students at the University of Pennsylvania. She referenced her husband's and 2005 speech, providing an addendum for those in the audience. "One of life's most beautiful dimensions is integrating those you have lost into your own being. We see more, we understand more. And we love more," she said.

* * *

Unlike some people my age, I look forward to my birthdays. Oh, no big-shebang party, not any bang really. But I do enjoy privately celebrating another year and look forward to the potential of another. Every year, my wife makes my favorite dessert of all time, cherry delight. It's my mom's recipe, and my wife follows the steps closely from the original recipe card written over 50 years ago in my tiny childhood kitchen. It seems like I love it more each year. I'm not sure if my growing appreciation is because of the sweetness of the cherries or my fondness for the memories. The recipe has not changed. I think I know.

Momma was right, death is part of life, a very important part. It reminds us that life is short and fragile. If there is something worth doing, do it now. And maybe, more important, it reminds us that relationships are an important part of life. We grow, we love, we are happy, and often, we postpone the very topic of this conversation. Yes, momma was a smart woman, and in some way, she will always be with us. Maybe it's in the simple sweetness of our favorite dessert. I will always love her Cherry Delight.

We Are All Gonna Die

It was another beautiful day on the lake. We were anchored in the deepest part of the bay, the kids were having a great time swimming, and I was absorbed in a good book so we didn't see the storm coming in fast from the west.

The sky suddenly opened up with a torrential downpour, the kind of rain that almost hurts as it hits your bare skin. Then a crack of thunder. We didn't see the lightning strike but from the loudness of the boom, we knew it had to be close. I pulled up the anchor and headed home as fast as we could.

"We are all gonna die," shouted my wafer-thin daughter, who was eight at the time, her long strawberry-blonde hair wet from the rain, but still blowing in the wind as I sped the boat to our dock. Yes, we are all gonna die, but just not today.

Death is not a comfortable topic to think about or talk about. Yet I chose to make you read about it again, a second conversation about death. But maybe it should be more comfortable.

Have you heard of a death café? At a death café, people, often strangers, drink tea, eat cake, and discuss death. The aim, according to the website, is to increase awareness of death and to help people make the most of their finite lives. I ask you, is anyone really not aware of death?

Since September 2011, there have been 16,056 pop-up cafés in over 85 countries (and counting), where people gather to talk about death. One of the cafés was organized by a group calling itself the Amateur's Guide to Death and Dying. I couldn't find a group whose members considered themselves to be experts, maybe for good reason.

They, the death café, did suggest that talk of death doesn't diminish the values of life. In many ways, it can enhance it with the understanding that life is finite. Again, we are grateful for the reminder. Ram Dass, in his book *Still Here: Embracing Aging, Changing, and Dying*, says, "We each bring to the moment of our passing the summation of all that we've lived and done, which is why we must begin as soon as possible to prepare . . . becoming the sort of people who can close their eyes for the last time without regrets." Regrets often come up in a conversation about death. I think we should talk about this.

We all carry regrets in our lives. It's just part of living. According to the experts, regrets are often associated with the choices and actions we didn't make: the careers we didn't pursue; the romance we didn't allow; or the simple call we didn't make. In most cases, we carry those regrets with us to the end.

Bronnie Ware, an Australian nurse and counselor who worked in palliative care, wrote a book in 2012 called *The Top Five Regrets of the Dying*. As part of her therapy, she would ask about regrets: if given a second chance, would you do something differently? She found five regrets that stood out and were most common among her dying patients:

1. I wish I had pursued my dreams and aspirations and not the life that others expected from me. The answer in life, she says, is to ask yourself, Will the other voices matter to you in your final days? A kind of deathbed assessment as you evaluate your options.

2. I wish I hadn't worked so hard. I have mixed emotions about this one. I'm a big fan of full effort in everything we do. But I do understand a life of balance and spending time with family and friends. I wonder if this would have been as big a regret if we were to solve the first regret.

3. I wish I had the courage to express my feelings and speak my mind. This one makes me sad. The solution seems so easy, but I understand why it's so hard.

4. I wish I had stayed in touch with my friends. Okay, please put this book down now and call or contact three old friends. We can fix this right here and now.

5. I wish I had let myself be happier. This one breaks my heart. I think it speaks to the confusion surrounding happiness.

Regret is a powerfully strong emotion that most people will feel at some time in their lives. In Daniel Pink's book *The Power of Regret: How Looking Backward Moves Us Forward*, only 1 percent of people report having no regrets.

Regret and disappointment arise when an outcome is not what you wanted, counted on, or thought would happen. But with disappointment, you often believe the outcome was outside of your control. This is why regret's such a powerful emotion. Yes, we believe the outcome was caused by our decision or actions, and the outcome was our fault.

Pink was the lead researcher for the American Regret Project. The research, conducted in June 2020, surveyed 4,489 Americans to collect their attitudes about regret. This is reportedly the largest pool of data ever collected on the subject, the results from which are organized into four basic categories:

1. Foundation regrets: Failure to be responsible, conscientious, or prudent. "If only I had done the work." Many financial, career, and health regrets can be found in this category.

2. Boldness regrets: Humans are much more likely to regret inaction, the chances they didn't take. The missed opportunities, career, chasing the love, learning a language, reconnecting with a friend. "If only . . . ." Inaction regrets were the most commonly reported type of regret.

3. Moral regrets: Those times when you had a choice and took the low road. "If only I had done the right thing." This is the smallest category of regret but often the most painful.

4. Connection regrets: When you neglected the people who matter to you. Humans have a massive amount of regret about fractured or unrealized relationships. "If only I had reached out." This regret is closely related to boldness regrets, but such an important regret deserved its own category. May I add, it's often the most easily fixed. (See my prompt earlier in this conversation.)

* * *

What about living a life with no regrets? It's an interesting question that's often sung about. Eminem crooned in "No Regrets," . . . You know, if I had a / chance to do it all / over again (Oh, oh) / I wouldn't change shit. And Mark Twain wrote, "Life is short, break the rules, forgive quickly, kiss slowly, love truly, laugh uncontrollably, and never regret anything that makes you smile." Don't ya love the attitude?

The "no regrets" ethos is strong, but as Daniel Pink points out, it can also be dangerous. "Regret is actually a marker of a healthy and maturing mind. At its essence, life's mistakes are powerful teachers, pointing us closer to what we really need and value."

For those regrets that still have an open door, make the call. For the others, it is okay to wonder what would have happened if . . . . But with or without regret, death is a wonderful reminder of how to live life.

Socrates, one of the greatest minds of all time, didn't fear death. He respected it. He felt that death shouldn't be dreaded or feared, because he had lived a good life. "Be of good cheer about death, and know this of a truth. That no evil can happen to a good man, either in life or after death." He spoke these words as he was about to be put to death for influencing the young people of the time. His words, "I cannot teach anyone anything, I can only teach them how to think," were not a popular mantra in his time.

Nobody in history has been more attuned to the power of death than the Stoics. They used thoughts of death as a tool to improve their outlook on life.

Marcus Aurelius, the most famous Stoic, once said, "Stop whatever you are doing and ask yourself: Am I afraid of death because I won't be able to do this anymore?" Wow, a dynamic way of evaluating our time.

In his essay "On the Shortness of Life," Seneca wrote, "Life is short, use your time wisely. Live each day with a sense of urgency and ask if we are focused on what's truly important. Prioritize being your highest self, your time is a precious commodity."

I have told my kids that I'm not afraid of death. To be clear, I'm terrified of the process of dying, which is usually not good. I fear crashing in a plane or sinking in a ship, but neither will stop me from my love of travel. I just take my Ambien and tough it out. Whatever my demise, I'm sure I will say for the final time, "I don't love this."

I'm not afraid to be dead though. My spiritual beliefs play a significant role in overcoming the fear. Seeing family and friends, in Heaven, has some appeal, even a happiness of sorts. The idea of having dinner with my parents again on the porch of their little white house feels very comforting. I just hope the invitation is not for this weekend or anytime soon.

ARE WE OLD YET?

I want to see my family live their lives. To watch my kids continue their journey and maybe someday see my grandkids. I have heard it's one of life's greatest joys. In one of my warped views of heaven, I will be tuning in on my giant screen to enjoy the action, flipping through all the family channels to take it all in. My joy of vicarious living will follow me into the next life. God, I hope reincarnation is not the plan. I don't want to be some bird having to fly between households. For that, I'm thankful I was raised Christian.

Like Socrates, I have lived life with a mantra, just not one that has led to my demise—at least not yet. For as long as I can remember, I have always told myself this phrase- Always happy, never satisfied. Now I fully understand there are some inherent issues with the phrase, as nobody can always be happy, and nobody is never satisfied. It was just a goal for the day to live as happily as possible but never too comfortable to stop striving for more. You don't have to like it, but it has worked for me.

My son claims that this is not an original phrase despite my ownership claim. Out of curiosity and not with the intent of proving my son wrong, I Googled it. And sure enough, he was (partially) right. Martial artist-actor Bruce Lee has been attributed with coining the phrase "Be happy, but never satisfied." Not exactly, but I won't be looking to trademark my phrase anytime soon. In defense of my originality, can I just say I have never been into karate. The closest I ever got was wearing Hai Karate aftershave in high school. We all did because it was cheap, and the TV commercials said it would make us irresistible to women. I stopped wearing it because it didn't work for me.

The mantra did help me get through life. My search for happiness was not of a hedonistic nature, most of the time, but it really did help me to be content and grateful and maintain a sense of well-being. The pursuit of satisfaction also helped in my pursuit of goals and kept me from being complacent.

* * *

All of this led to my second reason for not being afraid of death. I have lived a good life.

Jeff Bezos delivered the following words to Princeton graduates in 2010: "When you are 80 years old and in a quiet moment of reflection, narrating for only yourself the most personal of your life story, the telling that will be meaningful will be a series of choices that you made. In the end, we are our choices. Build yourself a great story."

I like my story so far, and it is not over. But enough about my death, let's talk about yours.

The Stoic concept memento mori, a reminder of mortality, seems like such a morbid way to live. For the Stoics, it was a simple way to remember to enjoy life and treasure more. Be more grateful for the simple things: the sun shining on your face, the shared laughs, and the luscious meals. It's a way to remind ourselves to never lose our zest for life.

Remember the phrase, or simply picture a little strawberry-blonde screaming at the top of her lungs, "We are all gonna die."

Enjoy your day.

Life Is a Highway

I have always loved to drive. I remember the freedom I felt at 16 years old, sitting behind the giant steering wheel of my 1966 white Dodge Coronet 440, thinking I could go anywhere. It was a gas-guzzler, only getting 11 miles per gallon (or there abouts), but I didn't care. With an open road ahead of me, it was just the beginning. The euphoria didn't last long. I quickly learned that the highway had rules, and if you didn't adhere to the rules, there would be consequences. Within three months of getting my license, I crashed into the back of a car waiting for the light to turn. Luckily no one was hurt; thank goodness I wasn't going fast because this was a time before seat belts. The accident was my fault, so I got a ticket for failing to stop within a clear distance. No shit. I hit the guy in front of me. I made a mistake. I paid for my mistake; I paid for the ticket. My license was restricted after I appeared before a judge. I was certain this wouldn't be my last mistake, but I learned from it and moved on down the highway.

Then came the first real road trip. The summer after high school graduation, my best friend and I traveled around Michigan. Up North, as we call it. No plans, no GPS, no reservations, just freedom that only comes once in our lives, or so we thought. We just drove, stopping when we wanted to, without a care, just the pursuit of . . . ? What were we pursuing? Fun, I guess. Yes, that was it. The highway would bring us a lifetime of fun or as much as we could handle.

Not always. Sometimes the highway can lead to disappointment. When I was a young boy, we were headed to the Cascades in Jackson, Michigan, a two-hour trip from home. We pulled in early in the day with the anticipated excitement of seeing the wonderful man-made waterfall, which was to be one of the highlights of the trip. When we arrived, all we saw was a bunch of giant dry bathtubs stacked on top of each other, but no waterfall. This was it, I thought. My first waterfall is a bunch of bathtubs. For a boy of eight, this was one of life's biggest disappointments, not understanding that there would be many roads in my future with far greater disappointments. Not long after this disappointment, on another road trip, I learned that life was not always fair. I'm not talking about the drivers that speed past us while we patiently wait in the merged line with upcoming construction, only for them to cut off the entire line at the last possible chance. They are just jerks, and there can be many jerks along the highway. No, this learning experience came as my family was traveling north through Ohio in our white Ford 500. This box of a car was so ugly, I think they paid us to remove it from the car lot, but I digress. (It was ugly but cheap.)

This road was heading home, which is always a good feeling. As we drove under an overpass under construction, some cement spattered on our car from above. I mean, what are the chances? Now our ugly family car just became uglier, with eight cement splats going from the front to the back of the car. I guess it could have been worse: we could have been driving a convertible. This type of could-have-been-worse reasoning helped me through a number of disappointments in my life.

As time moves on, the highway could become very monotonous. Driving to and from work each day in traffic is a good example. Each opportunity was a new drive and fun for a while because, well, it was new. But eventually not so much. Am I right? I always tried to make the best of it. New routes, listening to my favorite music, and in recent years, podcasts. Choose the best highway and make the best of it. This plan has worked well for me over the years.

At times the highway journey can be filled with the unexpected, such as unwanted construction or bad weather. These occurrences always seem to happen at the most inconvenient times. But actually, is there ever a good time for this? They cause us to slow down, create anxiety, and sometimes even cause us to change direction on our journey. But such is life. Learning to deal with the unexpected can make the rest of the journey so much better.

The best drives for me were often those that took me in new directions, provided new discoveries, and united me with family and friends. Roads that are different, some open, some crowded, but always interesting and full of beauty. We can find these roads even in our daily lives if we take the time to look.

Even after one of the long discovery road trips, there is something soothing when we get close to home. I know these roads, the curves, turns, blind spots, and even potholes to avoid. I know what to expect on these everyday roads, and there is something comforting in that.

We are all on the highways, but they are different in so many ways. Some of us have had more detours or bad weather to deal with; others have just simply been lost. Still others have been zipping along the autobahn their entire life. Whichever road we have been on, it hasn't been the highway that has determined our life but how we have driven on the highway. It has always been up to us.

My son started medical school last year, so he is on a super highway; the road is long, flat, and fast with a very clear destination. Very few off-ramps and rest stops along the way. A perfect road for him, but one that would be dull and boring for my daughter. Still in college (update- now has graduated, but does not change the story), she has not yet finalized her destination. So many exits and off-ramps that have a myriad of options and opportunities to explore and enjoy. Exits with Chick-fil-A or Culver's are her favorites.

I find the drive to be different now. It's not the highway; that has not changed. The difference is me. I'm driving a much older car. I have kept it in good shape to the point where some say, "Oh, I can't believe it's that old." To which I respond, "Thank you," but think, what do you mean "that old"? It's not that old. But it's the oldest car I've ever driven, and it makes noises—squeaks and rumbles—especially on those cold mornings. It works for me, and it's the only car I have.

I was thinking about my first car the other day, the Dodge Coronet 440. (Please forgive my lengthy reminiscing, that is what we do). They don't make cars with vinyl tops anymore. I paid $600 for that car and was wondering what it would be worth today. I used an inflation calculator to determine what that $600 would be worth today: $4,667.57.

I looked at Autotrader. I sorted my search results by price, with the cheapest showing at the top. First up was right around that price, coming in at $4,900. It would be best described as a Junker: rusted body, worn seats, bad tires, didn't run. I'm sure that the muffler didn't have glass packs, and worst of all, the radio didn't work.

The next three cars were a different story. They were well cared for, looked good, and ran. The price of each was about $25,000. Five times more than the value of my car half a century ago.

There was one more. This car was vintage and spotless, with all the extra features that made this car special. The asking price was $58,000.

All this builds up to make a point that getting old doesn't always lead to reduced value. Quite the contrary. The years add value if we are cared for (or care for ourselves) in the right way. By adding as many special features as possible, we can be vintage. I'm not old, I'm vintage. Still a great bumper sticker.

Our journey is not yet over. As long as there are highways, there is life to live.

Most of us know Rascal Flatts' version of the song "Life Is a Highway" because it was featured in the 2006 animated film

Cars. A fun movie, I might add. I saw it at the drive-in with my kids.

> Life is a highway
> I wanna drive it all night long

The song was actually written and first recorded in 1991 by Tom Cochrane, who was part of a band called Red Rider. Along with the other songs you have never heard from Red Rider was a non-hit called "No Regrets." Maybe this was meant to be a sequel to "Life Is a Highway," or at least in my metaphor, it works out that way with the closing lines giving us another life message:

> Might have seen better times
> Remember who you are, and don't you forget
> Oh, and have no, no regrets.

Enjoy your journey. Let's keep driving!

CONVERSATION 35

The Last Conversation

Here we are, the last conversation. At times I didn't think I would make it this far; you may have felt the same. I'm glad we both did.

I learned a great deal from writing this book. Mainly that getting old can be difficult, but it doesn't always have to be. We have far more influence on our journey than we once thought.

And I remembered that I love my memories. I have many, many wonderful memories. But there is so much I don't remember. I wish I had more pictures, started to journal much sooner, and had a bigger memory box.

In this final conversation, I have a few unrelated thoughts I would like to share to wrap things up. I hope you don't mind.

First, I have a confession to make. I wrote this entire book with a pencil, actually multiple pencils. I know this makes me sound . . . old, but I don't care. One of the many benefits of being old is not caring what others think of you. It's a freeing feeling.

Granted, this made the process take much longer, but I just think better with a pencil in my hand. But I didn't use just any pencil. I used the best pencil in the world, a Dixon Ticonderoga No. 2 pencil. And if you don't believe my claim, just look at their package, "The World's Best Pencil."

Ticonderoga pencils are made with premium cedar from well-managed forests and have latex-free erasers. When I write, it lays down just the perfect amount of graphite for easy reading. According to Dixon, one pencil should last for 45,000 words. I must press hard or have written larger-than-average words because I used more than a dozen pencils, not the one and a half pencils I should have used (according to their estimate).

In some strange way, pencils remind me of life. Pencils, like us, have a finite time in this world. The evidence of aging is rather obvious; pencils get shorter, and we look different. The shortened pencil needs to be held a little tighter but still manages to lay down graphite on the paper just like it did when first taken out of the package. Still useful until the end.

The eraser is a perfect reminder that it's fine to make mistakes. Take action, get it on paper, and if you don't like it, use the eraser and simply change it.

Admittedly, pencils are not that different from one another. But you know what else? People aren't that different. We share 99.9 percent of identical DNA. For the remaining 0.1 percent, the variations include single nucleotide polymorphisms, insertions, deletions, and structural variations. The 0.1 percent makes us unique. What's also different is how we use our life and what we leave behind.

One of the many notable works by Salvador Dalí was created solely in pencil. The emotional imagery tells the story of a complicated family history. The name of the piece is *Portrait of My Dead Brother.*

Many of the greatest speeches in history started as pencil drafts on paper. Speeches by Abraham Lincoln, Winston Churchill, and Reverend Martin Luther King Jr. changed the world.

It's what we leave behind, have shared with others—that's what's different, and important. Additionally, people and pencils both celebrate the aging process. On the Ticonderoga package is an anniversary logo with the words "Celebrating over 100 years of excellence." Congrats to them.

I called my brother last year on his birthday. He just turned 70. Naturally, I asked him in my most smart-ass kind of way, "How does it feel to be old?" Mind you, he's only two years older than I am, but he is old. I'm not.

He had an interesting response. "It feels good. I played softball twice this week, pickleball yesterday, did my daily swim, and was about to make a healthy salad for lunch." Living his best life. But his next statement was the one that made the light turn on for me. "I feel proud of my age. Not everybody gets to be this old." He said it as if he won some sort of trophy, or he should be wearing some sort of button, "Celebrating 70 years." Maybe he should.

It's funny—this aging-journey thing. When we are young, we want to be older. We are not just eight years old, we are eight and a half. At some point, we begin to feel differently about this growing older idea. Birthday celebrations become smaller, if they happen at all, and our age starts to become cryptic. "I'm 49-plus." What? Despite of our desire to hide our years, we do want the journey to continue.

My 50-year class reunion will be here soon. I'm on the planning committee, and we are finalizing the details. We wanted to keep the price low because guests are on a fixed income. That means meatballs, not roast beef. The committee voted down having a DJ because it would be too loud, people need to hear, and they won't dance anyway. I disagreed. During the brief program, we are going to read the names of the classmates who have passed. Each presenter will read the names of ten people who weren't able to celebrate with us. It will require eight presenters; our graduating class had 640 students.

And yes, there will be name tags. Because without them, we may not know who we were talking to. To begin with, we may not recognize them, and we will likely forget their name by the end of the conversation. So much has changed in 50 years.

We graduated from high school in 1973. The same year Bob Dylan wrote the song "Forever Young." Almost a prophetic anthem, although I didn't know it at the time. Let me share just a few lines, although I would encourage you to listen to the entire song for a full nostalgic affect.

> May your wishes all come true.
> May your heart always be joyful.
> May you stay forever young.

Our reunion will be a wonderful time to relive our past. "What's new since I last saw you last, 50 years ago?" It almost doesn't seem real. I also hope to ask, "What's next? What are your plans for the future?" Maybe this will be an even better conversation.

Our planning committee decided that this will be our last formal reunion. There will likely be just small get-togethers in future years. We didn't say it, but the underlying reason for the decision was that we knew the odds of getting a large group together again were less likely.

So are we old? Did we ever gain consensus to answer the question in the title of this book? No, we didn't because there is no consensus. The answer is up to you. And whatever your answer is, you would be correct. It's one more beautiful thing about being our age- we decide.

As for me, I'm less worried about the years. Oh, don't get me wrong, I do want to live a bunch more, and I'm enjoying some healthy living to get me there. But someday, I will again start having chocolate milkshakes every night before I go to bed. Just not tonight. Tonight I'll drink my green tea; thank God for my family, friends, and my health; and sleep for eight hours.

Tomorrow I will (hopefully) wake up, grab a wonderful cup of coffee and do whatever I can to have my "first best day ever."

Enjoy.

RESOURCES

Akshay, Bareja. September 6, 2019. Frontiers in Cell Development Biology. "Maximizing Longevity and Healthspan."

Armstron, Sue. November 2, 2020. Science Focus. "Forever Young: Senescent Cells And Secret To Stopping Aging."

Arthur, Amy. June 23, 2022. BBC Science Focus. "Turtles Have Figured Out How To Stop Aging-Why Can't We?"

Barker, Eric. April 28, 2019. Ladders. "This Is How To Have A Long Awesome Life: 7 Secrets From Research."

Barth, Diane LCSW. September 21, 2014. Psychology Today. "5 Ways to Find Balance in Your Life."

Basaraba, Sharon. February 13, 2023. VeryWell Health. "Chronological vs. Biological Age."

Bateman, Tom. December 14, 2021. Euronews.next. "Can We Live Forever? New Anti-Ageing Vaccine Could Bring Immortality One Step Closer."

Bengtson, Vern PhD. November 22, 2014. The Gerontologist. "From Ageism To The Longevity Revolution."

Berg, Sara. January 26, 2023. AMA. "Massive Study Uncovers How Much Exercise Is Needed To Live Longer."

Berghoff, Maren. August 29, 2022. Neuroscience News. "Brief Exposure To Rapamycin Has The Same Anti-Aging Effects As Lifelong Treatment."

Berman, Robby. December 20, 2022. Medical News Today. "Study Identifies Unique Set Of Attributes To Healthy, Optimal Aging."

Berns-Zare, Ilene PsyD. December 6, 2022. Psychology Today. "What Are The Secret Ingredients To Happiness."

Bertolotti, JW. September 29, 2022. Medium. "Three Reasons To Meditate On Your Mortality- Like Marcus Aurelius."

Birch, Jenna. September 16, 2020. Well+Good. "The Habits For Longevity That Most Resonate With You. According To Myers-Briggs."

Blanding, Michael. May 26, 2021. The Harvard Gazette. "Aging Matters."

Borji, H.S. August 9, 2021. Investopia. "4 Global Economic Issues Of An Aging Population."

Boyan, Nicolas. 2022. IPSOS. "Global Happiness Study."

Breines, Juliana PhD. May 2, 2023. Psychology Today. "4 Ways To Find Happiness When Life Doesn't Turn Out As Planned."

Bresnahan, Samantha. November 30, 2018. CNN Health. "You Have Two Ages, Chronological and Biological. Here's Why It Matters."

Brooks, Arthur. October 10, 2022. Peter Attia Podcast. "The Science Of Happiness."

Brower, Tracy PhD. August 22, 2021. Forbes. "The Power Of Purpose And Why It Matters Now."

Brown, Dawn Dr. July 21, 2021. Forbes. "How To Build Your Identity In Na d Out Of Work."

Bruno, Beth. July 13, 2022. Medium. "Things People Never Say On Their Deathbed."

Buettner, Dan. July 7, 2016. National Library of Medicine. "Blue Zones."

Buettner, Dan. September 2009. Ted. "How To Live To Be 100."

Buettner, Dan. July 7, 2016. American Journal of Lifestyle Medicine. "Blue Zones."

Buford, Bob. Halftimeinstitute.org. "Halftime Report."

Butler, Robert MD. December 2014. Gerontologist. "From Ageism To The Longevity Revolution."

Byrne, Jessica. July 4, 2022. Thred. "Drug That Increases Human Lifespan To 200 Years Is In The Works."

Campbell, Judy. May 23, 2022. Guava. "6 Methods Scientists Are Exploring To Slow Aging."

Chen, Zheng. May 27, 2023. Neuroscience News. "Gene Therapy Reverses Age-Related Hearing Loss."

Cherry, Kendra MSEd. June 28, 2021. VeryWellmind. "Using Learned Optimism In Your Life."

Christianson, K. PhD. February 11, 1999. National Library of Medicine. "A Danish Population- Based Twin Study On General Health In The Elderly."

Christianson, Matt. April 29, 2021. Fatherly. "12 Important Questions To Ask Your Dad Before He's Gone."

Claus, Patricia. September 28, 2022. Greek Reporter. "Socrates' Views on Death Will Help You Deal With Fear."

Cobb, Cynthia. June 18, 2019. Healthline. "How To Live Your Best Life As You Age."

Cuasay, Maria Nina. Activeman. "Reverse Aging 101:Shocking Breakthroughs Of Science And Future Possibilities."

Curtin, Melanie. Inc. "Yale Researcher's Say Doing This Simple Activity Can Add 2 Years To Your Life."

Datz, Todd. June 8, 2022. Harvard School Of Public Health. "High Optimism Linked With Longer Life And Living Past 90."

Davidson, Helen. March 3, 2015. The Guardian. "Which Are The Best Countries in The World to Grow Old In?"

Davis, Daniel. February 6, 2022. Big Think. "Jeff Bezos Is Looking To Defy Death."

Davis, Daniel. January 29, 2022. The Conversation. "How A Major Aging Breakthrough Could Dramatically Extend Human Longevity."

Davis, Matt. August 20, 2019. Big Think. "8 Ways To Achieve Self-Actualization."

Davis, Paula. February 8, 2022. Forbes. "Do You Wish You Had Done Things Differently? The Four Categories of Regret."

Davis, Tchiki Ph.D. May 24, 2021. Psychology Today. "4 Tips To Be More Optimistic."

Dawson, Alene. John Templeton Foundation. "A Conversation With Professor Robert Waldinger on 'The Good Life' Study Of Happiness."

Degges-White, Suzanne Ph.D. October 15, 2021. Psychology Today. "Personal and Social Identity: Who Are You Through Others Eyes."

Demmer, Jenna. August 10, 2021. Health Digest. "The Surprising Day You're Most Likely To Die."

Diamandis, Peter. April 15, 2022. Fast Company. "Anti-Aging Technology Is Coming."

Ditchen, Stephanie. October, 16, 2019. The Harvard Gazette. "Scientists PinPoint Neural Activity's Role In Human Longevity."

Dus, Monica PhD. March 1, 2022. The Conversation. "What You Eat Can Reprogram Your Genes."

Edmond, Charlotte. September 17, 2019. World Economic Forum.

"Elderly People Make Up A Third Of Japan's Population."

Eisenberg, Richard. October 18, 2022. Marketwatch. "Retirement Can Mean A Loss Of Identity- How To Bring Happiness To Your Next Act."

Ferlita, Gabriella. August 2, 2022. Unilad. "Japan Has an 'Island of Immortals' Where Average Age is Incredibly High and Disease is Very Low."

Ferrari, Nick. March 1, 2017. AARP. "50 Ways To Live A Longer, Healthier Life."

Fetell-Lee, Ingrid. April 27, 2021. Ideas.TED.com. "Aging Is Inevitable, So Why Not Do It Joyfully?"

Fleming, Kevin. July 7, 2003. National Library of Medicine. "A Cultural and Economic History Of Old Age In America."

Foebel, Andrea D. PhD. April 5, 2016. National Library of Medicine. "Genetic Influences On Functional Capacities In Aging."

Gagliani, Michelle. March 9, 2021. The Balanced CEO. "The 8 Elements of a Balanced Life."

Garcia, Hector. Book. *Ikigai.*

Garth, Elenor. January 27, 2023. Longevity Technology. "A Decade Of Research Expands The Hallmarks Of Aging From Nine To Twelve."

Garth, Elenor. May 25, 2023. Longevity Technology. "Oxygen Restriction Enhances Lifespan Of Rapidly Aging Mice."

George, Bojan MA Law. December 31, 2022. The Collector. "How The Stoics Found Calm by Contemplating Death."

Gepp, Karin PsyD. January 26, 2022. Psych Central. "Does Your Personality Change With Age? Science Says Yes."

Gholamnedjad, Hanieh PhD. May 2019. "Self-Actualization: Self-Care Outcomes Among Elderly."

Graeden, Ellie. October 22, 2022. "An Aging Population Needs A Different Approach To Housing And Care."

Greenspan, Jesse. April 2, 2013. "The Myth Of Ponce de Leon And The Fountain Of Youth."

Greenwood, Veronique. March 10, 2011. "The Longevity Project: Decades Of Data Reveal Paths To Long Life."

Grogan, Jessica PhD. 2013. Encountering Maslow.

Gwynne, Peter. January 17, 2017. "Here's How Far Cryonic Preservation Has Come."

Haden, Jeff. July 11, 2018. "This 95-Year Stanford Study Reveals 1 Secret To Living A Longer, More Fulfilling Life."

Hall, John. April 10, 2019. "A 30-Year Harvard Study Reveals The 5 Simple Habits That May Prolong Your Life By 10 Years Or More."

Hamczyk, Magda PhD. March 3, 2020. "Biological Versus Chronological Aging."

Hammon, Claudia. July 22, 2022. "Can You Delay Ageing by Refusing to Act Your Age."

Headley, CW. August 22, 2021. "Two Brain Functions Actually Improve With Age."

Headley, CW. May 12, 2020. "According To Science, This Is The Age That Means You Are Officially Old."

Herpen, Robert. October 25, 2022. "Optimism In Older Adults Improves Recovery After Stroke."

Hodges, Richard M.D. "Strategic Directions for Research 2020-2025."

Hogan, Matt. November 1, 2017. "Happy But Never Satisfied."

Holcombe, Madeline. November 29, 2022. "Why Most Men Don't Have Enough Close Friends."

Holiday, Ryan. February 22, 2022. The Medium. "19 Rules For A Better Life (From Marcus Aureius)."

Horton, Brierley. June 1, 2021. Livestrong.com. "If You Want To Age Well, This May Be The Most Important Habit To Stick With."

Houser, Kristen. May 27, 2021. Freethink. "Human Lifespan May Have A Hard Limit: 150 Years."

Huber, Jeff. August 20, 2018. LinkedIn. "Five Ways to Make the Most of Life After 50."

Icekson, Tamar. February 28, 2014. National Institute on Aging. "Effects Of Optimism On Creativity Under Approach And Avoidance Motivation."

Ireland, Tom. January 12, 2020. BBC Science Focus. "Wild Ideas In Science: There's An Off-Switch For Aging."

Irving, Michael. December 2, 2020. New Atlas. "New Evidence Strengthens Link Between Telomere Length, Aging And Cancer."

Irving, Paul. March 10, 2021. Next Avenue. "The Future Of Aging: What 20 Experts Told Us."

Issak, Adam. February 23, 2020. CNBC. "The Ultra-Rich Are Investing In Companies Trying To Reverse Aging."

Jaffe-Hoffman, Maayan. November 22, 2020. The Jerusalem Post. "Israeli Scientist Claim To Reverse Aging Process."

Jlaototong, Xi'an. June 1, 2022. Sci Tech Daily. "Stanford Scientists Discover That Adding a Particular Seafood To Your Diet Can Reverse Signs of Aging."

Johnson, Steven. July 20, 2021. Fast Company. "A Short History Of How We've Ended Up Living So Much Longer."

Journal Article. January 14, 2015. The Commonwealth Fund. "Medicare At 50-Origins And Evolution."

Kaeberlein, Matt Ph.D. August 6, 2018. National Library of Medicine. "Challenges in Defining Healthspan."

Karasawa, Mayumi. July 29, 2011. Sage Journals. "Cultural Perspectives On Aging And Well-Being."

Karp, Hannah. August 29, 2011. The Wall Street Journal. "Novak Djokovic's Secret: Sitting In A Pressurized Egg."

Kavedzija, Iza MD. Bluezones.com. "The Japanese Concept Of Ikigai-Why Purpose Might Be A Better Goal Than Happiness."

Kaysen, Ronda. December 7, 2018. AARP. "The Truth About Grumpy Old Men."

Kent, Lauren. March 28, 2022. CNN Health. "Nostagia Can Reduce Perception Of Pain, Study Shows."

Kershner, Jim. August 5, 2013. The Spokesmen Review. "The Reasons Behind Grumpy Old Man Syndrome."

Kika, Thomas. December 12, 2021. Newsweek. "Japanese Scientists Claim Vaccine Removes Zombie Cells Behind "Aging Related Diseases.""

Kirkland, James. April 11, 2017. eBiomedicine. "Cellular Senescence: A Translational Perspective."

Koenig, Harold. December 16, 2012. ISRN Psychiatry. "Religion, Spirituality, And Health: The Research And Clinical Implications."

LaMotte, Sandee. January 13, 2023. CNN Health. "Old Mice Grow Young Again In Study. Can People Do The Same."

Landry, Roger. Book.

Lanese, Nicoletta. October 28, 2022. Live Science. "Zombie Cells In The Body Tied To Aging May Actually Help Heal Tissue Damage."

Larson, Vicki. June 23, 2022. Medium. "I'm 65-Am I officially 'Old?'"

Laurence, Emily. October 5, 2019. Well & Good. "The Longest Living People In The World Have These 9 Things In Common."

Leamey, Taylor. March 20, 2023. CNET. "Cultivate Your Happiness With These 7 Daily Habits."

Lee, Ingrid. April 27, 2021. Ideas.TED.com. "Aging is Inevitable, So Why Not Do It Joyfully?"

Lee, Ruby. May 23, 2021. Medium. "Ten Reasons Why Getting Old Sucks."

Lehpamer, Nicole. September 27, 2022. Mather Institute. "Mind Of Matter: Perceptions Of Aging Are A Self Fulfilling Prophecy."

Lincoln, GA. July 13, 2001. National Library of Medicine. "The Irritable Male Syndrome."

Linden, Ingemar Patrick. May 30, 2022. The MIT Press. "A Philosopher's Case Against Death."

Liotta, Dennis MD. February 18, 2020. LinkedIn. "Maslow's Hierarchy Of Needs Flips Over For The Elderly."

Liu, Xiaosong. December 18, 2008. National Library of Medicine. "Yamanaka Factors Critically Regulate Developmental Signaling."

Lockhart, Emily. March 16, 2015. ActiveBeat. "Age-Defying Lifestyle Changes."

Loh, Matthew. August 30, 2022. Insider. "Scientists Have Mapped the Genetic Code of the Immortal Jellyfish."

Lopez-Otin, Carlos PhD. June 6, 2013. National Library of Medicine. "The Hallmarks Of Aging."

Lorenzetti, Laura. March 7, 2016. Fortune. "The Obsession With Curing Aging Is Now Big Business."

Lyubomirsky, Sonja. 2005. Published Paper. "Cultivate Your Happiness With These 7 Daily Habits."

Macpherson, Greg. Book. *Harnessing the Nine Hallmarks of Aging*

Malito, Alessandra. November 18, 2018. Barron's. "Harvard Scientists Say These 5 Things Can Prolong Your Life By A Decade."

Manley, Alex. June 20, 2023. Ask Men. "The Importance Of Close Friendships For Men."

Mantzioris, Evaneline. September 21, 2022. The Conversation. "What's The Longevity Diet, And Will It Really Make You Live Longer?"

March, David. November 6, 2022. Neuroscience News. "Lucid Dying: Patients Recall Death Experience During CPR."

Martinez-Carter. Karina. January 10, 2015. The Week. "How The Elderly are Treated Around The World."

Mazanec, Tara. November 4, 2012. Life Hack. "Think Getting Old Sucks? Here's Why Aging Doesn't Have To Suck."

McLeod, Saul PhD. July 7, 2023. Simply Psychology. "Maslow's Hierarchy Of Needs Flips Over For The Elderly."

McNicoll, Geoffrey. March 23, 2020. Wiley Online Library. "Warren C. Sanderson and Sergei Scherbov Prospective Longevity."

Meck, Chloe. January 6, 2023. Neuroscience News. "How Exercise Preserves Physical Fitness During Aging."

Mehta, Divit. July 14, 2022. Medium. "Seneca: On The Shortness Of Life Summarized."

Melkonian, Lois. February 11, 2021. BetterUp. "What Is Emotional Well-Being? 8 Ways To Improve Mental Health."

Mellardo, Alexa. October 11, 2022. Eat This, Not That! "The 5 Wellness Habits That Slow Down Aging, Science Reveals."

Menting, Ann Marie. September 1, 2021. Harvard Medicine. "A Conversation on Aging Research."

Migala, Jessica. March 23, 2021. Livestrong.com. "4 Habits This Octogenarian Aging Expert Does Every Day for Longevity."

Mikhail, Alexa. January 14, 2023. Fortune. "Researchers Have Followed 700 People To Find Keys To Happiness."

Milstein, Marc. November 22, 2022. CNBC. "Brain Expert: The No. 1 Thing That Sets 'Super Agers' Apart."

Mineo, Liz. April 11, 2017. The Harvard Gazette. "Good Genes Are Nice, But Joy Is Better."

Mlynaryk, Nicole. March 21, 2023. Neuroscience News. "To Ward Off Aging, Stem Cells Must Take Out The Trash."

Molteni, Megan. October 21, 2019. Wired. "A New Crisper Technique Could Fix Almost All Genetic Diseases."

Morgan, Kate. April 13, 2021. BBC Worklife. "Why We Define Ourselves By Our Jobs."

Murphy, Bill. February 6, 2023. Inc. "An 80-Year Harvard Study Found The Secret To A Happy Life."

Narvaez, Darcia PhD. June 30, 2019. Psychology Today. "Self-Actualization And Becoming A Wise Elder."

Nazeri, Haleh. January 19, 2023. World Economic Forum. "Why Longevity Literacy Is The Secret To A Prosperous Long Life."

Nealon, Cory. November 15, 2022. Brighter Side Of News. "Incredible Protein Can Reverse Muscle Aging , New Research Finds."

Neighmond, Patti. September 1, 2019. NPR. "Optimists For The Win: Finding The Bright Side Might Help You Live Longer."

Newcomb, Tim. January 10, 2023. Popular Mechanics. "Scientists Just Reprogrammed Mice To Live Longer. Humans May Be Next."

Nikolova, Milena. May 2, 2016. Brookings. "Two Solutions To Challenges Of Population Aging."

Nome, Valerie. January 28, 2023. Apple News. "Wealthy Entrepreneur Reversed His Biological Age With A $2 Million Treatment Program."

O'Brian, Sharon. March 17, 2018. Liveabout.com. "When Does Old Begin?"

Offord, Catherine. January 13, 2023. Science Focus. "Two Research Teams Reverse Signs Of Aging In Mice."

Onken, Orrin. August 10, 2022. Medium. "Is Every Age the Best Age to Be?"

O'Reilly, Matthew. Ted Talks. "'Am I Dying?' The Honest Answer."

Paredes, Jim. January 19, 2014. PhilStar Global. "How To Avoid Becoming Grumpy As We Age."

Park, Alice. January 12, 2023. Time. "Scientists Have Reached A Key Milestone in Learning How To Reverse Aging."

Park, Alice. January 8, 2020. Time. "Scientists Calculated How Much Longer You Can Live With A Healthy Lifestyle."

Parker, John. The Economist. "The Decade Of The Old Begins."

Partridge, Linda. January 12, 2011. The Royal Society. "The New Science Of Ageing."

Pederson, Dorthe PhD. December 22, 2019. National Library of Medicine. "The Danish Twin Registry."

Pederson, Nancy. July 2017. eBioMedicine. "Biological Age Predictors."

Pinker, Susan. 2017. Ted. "The Secret To Living Longer May Be Your Social Life."

Pistilli, Melissa. February 22, 2023. Investing News. "5 US Anti-Aging Stocks."

Pomeroy, Ross. December 5, 2022. Neuropsych. "We All Can Reach A 'Flow State.'"

Powell, Alvin. January 30, 2023. The Harvard Gazette. "Has First Person To Live To Be 150 Been Born?"

Ratini, Melinda MS, DO. August 4, 2021. Web MD. "What To Expect In Your 70's."

Regalado, Antonio. January 9, 2023. MIT Technology Review. "The Biotech Startup Says Mice Love Longer After Genetic Reprogramming."

Regalado, Antonio. June 7, 2022. MIT Technology Review. "Saudi Arabia Plans To Spend $1 Billion A Year Discovering Treatment To Slow Aging."

Regalado, Antonio. MIT Technology Review. "How Scientists Want To Make You Young Again."

Regan, Sarah. October 30, 2022. mbgmindfulness. "9 Ways To Find Your Passion At Any Age, According To Experts."

Restak, Richard. February 2, 2023. CNBC. "An 81-Year-Old Brain Doctor's 7 Hard Rules For Keeping Memory Sharp As A Whip."

Richter, Felix. February 22, 2023. World Economic Forum. "The World's Oldest Populations."

Rickles, Dean. Book. *Life Is Short: Guide To Making It More Meaningful.*

Roberts, Brent PhD. 2018. Psych Central. "Does Personality Change With Age?"

Robertson, Ruairi PhD. August 29, 2017. Healthline. "Why People in Blue Zones Live Longer Than The Rest Of The World."

Robson, David. May 25, 2015. BBC News. "What's the Prime of Your Life."

Rosenberg, Eric. March 16, 2023. Investopia. "How Does The French Retirement Age Stack Up Globally?"

Routledge, Clay PhD. January 14, 2020. Frontiers In Psychology. "Why Meaning In Life Matters For Societal Flourishing."

Rura, Nicole. July 12, 2022. The Harvard Gazette. "Spirituality Linked With Better Health Outcomes, Patient Care."

Ryder, Gina. January 26, 2022. PsychCentral. "Does Personality Change With Age?"

Sales, Nancy Jo. July 24, 2022. The Guardian. "I Love Being 57."

Sample, Ian. February 8, 2023. The Guardian. "Anti-Aging Scientists Extend Lifespan Of Oldest Living Lab Rat."

Santos, Laurie PhD. 2022. Yale. "The Science Of Well-Being."

Schmauck-Medina. Thomas PhD. August 29, 2022. National Library of Medicine. "New Hallmarks Of Aging."

Schultz, Marc. January 25, 2023. Big Think. "What Decades Od Research Tells Us About Living The Good Life."

Schwab, Klaus. January 18, 2022. World Economic Forum. "David Sinclair Explains What An Aging Population Means For Economies Around The World."

Scuderi, Royale. September 26, 2022. LifeHack. "10 Simple Ways to Find Balance and Get Your Life Back."

Seaton Jefferson, Robin. October 29, 2019. Forbes. "What 71, 000 Americans Did To Help Them Live Longer."

Shaevitz, Morton Ph.D. June 1, 2016. Psychology Today. "How To Avoid Being A Grumpy Old Man (Or Woman)."

Shortsleeve, Cassie. March 26, 2023. Men's Health. "How Testosterone Effects Your Lifespan."

Shoven, John Ph.D. October 15, 2007. SSRN. "New Age Thinking: Alternative Ways Of Measuring Age."

Sinclair, David. January 18, 2022. World Economic Forum. "David Sinclair Explains What An Aging Means For Economies Around The World."

Skrobonja, Brian. May 21, 2021. Kiplinger. "Living A Life Of Purpose After Retirement: 3 Action Steps To Take."

Sohn, Lydia. July 3, 2019. CNBC. "What Do 90-Somethings Regret Most?"

Spivack, Elana. August 30, 2021. Inverse. "Scientists Discover One Kind Of Friend Is Best For Brain Health."

Staff. Psychology Today. "Gratitude."

Staff. A Train Education. "Irritable Male Syndrome."

Staff. University Of Minnesota. "The Perception And Experience Of Aging."

Staff. December 11, 2020. National Council On Aging. "The Background and History of The Older Americans Act."

Staff. Macrotrends. "U.S. Life Expectancy 1050-2023."

Staff. October 28, 2021. Medical News. "25 Common Habits That Make People Age Faster."

Staff. American Federation For Aging Research. "The Tame Trial: Targeting The Biology Of Aging."

Staff. Mayo Clinic. "Aging: What To Expect."

Staff. March 15, 2019. Good Therapy. "Achieve Self-Actualization."

Staff. March 15, 2023. Neuroscience News. "The Science Behind Memory."

Staff. January 19, 2023. Neuroscience News. "Why Do We Remember Emotional Events Better Than Non-emotional Ones?"

Staff. December 8, 2022. National Institute on Aging. "Optimism Linked To Longevity And Well-Being In Two Recent Studies."

Staff. May 25, 2018. Mayo Clinic. "Senescent Cells: Promising Anti-Aging Targets For Health Span."

Staff. Daily Stoic. "12 (Stoic) Rules For Life: An Ancient Guide To The Good Life."

Staff. Wikipedia. "What Would Jesus Do?"

Staff. March 20, 2021. For Seniors. "At What Age Is Someone Considered Elderly?"

Staff. February 2014. AARP. "AARP Attitudes Of Aging Study.

Staff. UN. "Older Person."

Staff. Openstax. "Who Are The Elderly?"

Staff. The Institute for Functional Medicine. "Measuring Age: Steve Horvath, PhD, And Epigenetic Clocks."

Staff. January 20, 2020. Excellence Reporter. "R. Buckminster Fuller: On The Wisdom And The Purpose Of Life."

Staff. March 15, 2023. Neuroscience News. "The Science Behind Memory."

Staloch, Laura. October 30, 2022. PsyPost. "Feeling Low? Take A Walk Down Memory Lane."

Steele, Andrew. January 1, 2023. Wired. "A Drug To Treat Aging May Not Be A Pipedream."

Steele, Andrew. December 27, 2020. The Telegraph. "The New Science Of Aging-And How To Stay Young For Longer."

Steele, Andrew. March 17, 2021. BBC Science Focus. "The Race To Stop Ageing: 10 Breakthroughs That Will Help Us Grow Old Healthily."

Stein, Samantha Psy.D. December 10, 2022. Psychology Today. "An Attitude of Gratitude."

Stibich, Mark PhD. March 17, 2022. VeryWell Health. "Real Age Longevity Calculator Review."

Stillman, Jessica. April 19, 2022. Inc. "A New Study Suggests A Way To Raise Your Life Expectancy By 5 Years."

Strecher, Vic PhD. 2022. University Of Michigan. "Finding Purpose and Meaning In Life."

Strecher, Vic PhD. Coursera. "Finding Purpose And Meaning In Life: Living For What Matters Most."

Strgatz, Steven. July 27, 2022. Quanta Magazine. "Why Do We Get Old and Can Aging Be Reversed."

Sullivan, Danny. May 16, 2023. Longevity Technology. "Does SIRT6 Hold The Key To Longevity."

Sutherlin, Margaret. February 23, 2023. Bloomberg. "Will Humans Live To 150? Science Is Working On It."

Taylor, Chris. 2019. Mashable.com. "The End Of Aging."

Triggle, Nick. October 4, 2019. BBC News. "Why Aren't We Living Longer."

Tucker, Howard. April 11, 2023. CNBC. "At 100 Years Old, I'm The World's Oldest Practicing Doctor."

Ungar, Laura. August 31, 2022. Associated Press. "Zombie Cells Are Central to the Quest for Active, Vital Old Age."

Wagner, Gina. January 23, 2019. Men's Journal. "100 Ways To Live To 100."

Watson, Joey. June 25, 2021. ABC News. "Silicon Valley Is Trying To Cure Old Age."

Weiner, Jonathan. October 20, 2022. MIT Technology Review. "The Pursuit Of Immortality Is Getting Older. So Are We."

Weintraub, Karen. March 31, 2022. USA Today. "The Map Of Our DNAIs Finally Complete. Here's What That Means For Humanity."

Wilson, John Frederick. January, 25, 2023. Phys Org. "Death And Dying: How Different Cultures Deal With Grief And Mourning."

Wright, Josh. December 13, 2022. Behavior Scientist. "What Is The Power Of Regret? A Conversation With Daniel Pink."

Yilmaz, Eser Ph.D. Berkley Well-Being Institute. "Identity: Definition, Types, & Examples."

Zhavoronkov, Alex PhD. August 11, 2021. Forbes. "Aging Brings Us Closer to Death. Why Do We Get Happier As We Age?"

Zilber, Ariel. January 26, 2023. News.com.au. "Tech Mogul Bryan Johnson, 45, spends $2 Million Each Year To Get 18-Year-Old Body."